THE SOCIAL MEDIA
ACTION PLAN

Ajay Tejwani

The Social Media Action Plan

Social Media Sapiens

3463 Magic Drive

San Antonio, TX 78229

DEDICATION

To my wife, Pooja,

and my wonderful daughters, Akeila and Nikita

ACKNOWLEDGMENTS

Lisa Baehr – Initial editing

Lillie Ammann – Final editing

Lyn Ceniza – Cover design

Brandon Kreager – Cover design

TABLE OF CONTENTS

CHAPTER 1: WHAT IS WORD OF MOUTH?

WORD OF MOUTH

In simple words, word of mouth means people providing information to other people based on their experience with a product or a service. We all have experienced, and believed, word of mouth at some time or the other.

Think about the last time you travelled to a new place. Whom did you consult before going: friends, family, online ratings and reviews, websites? We will all ask our family and friends if they have visited your travel destination to try to learn from their experiences and make our own trip most enjoyable.

The same things you heard about places and attractions that made you finally decide that you should or should not go to those places holds true for your business as well. When people are having conversations (which they will have anyway) about your brand, they are sharing their experiences with their family, friends, and the whole world. So, this is the nutshell of this chapter: Word of Mouth is an integral part of any business—it's just time to recognize it and make it a part of company strategy.

> *TIP:* All businesses (big or small) started with word of mouth, and some of the businesses lose that focus as they become bigger.

WHAT IS WORD OF MOUTH?

Word of mouth (also known as *viva voce*) refers to oral communication and the passing of information from person to person. Storytelling is the oldest form of word-of-mouth communication where one person tells others of something whether a real event or something made up.

~ *Source*: http://en.wikipedia.org/wiki/Word_of_mouth

People love to chat about things to show their knowledge, expertise, wisdom, allegiance, smartness etc. So, in today's communication world, you don't want to do the talking but let people talk to each other about your company's product or services.

Quite a few companies are built on Word of Mouth (WOM), but sometimes with time, growth, and day-to-day operations, we tend to forget how we started our company.

Marketing and public relations are controlled by journalists, TV commercials, radio jockeys, newspapers, and magazines. *The heart of any business is still WOM.* As the world becomes more social, relationships (not just innovative products and services) will be the key to success.

WOM is fundamental to any business, and acknowledging and harnessing that power will keep your business ahead of your competitors. The more people can talk about you (or with you), the more engaged they will be with your brand.

> *TIP*: Word of Mouth is the next best thing after face-to-face conversation, and the rules of both conversations remain the same: honest, authentic, and, finally, real-time that leaves a lasting impression of trust and integrity.

WHY WOULD PEOPLE TALK ABOUT YOU?

For this let me take you to the Maslow's hierarchy:

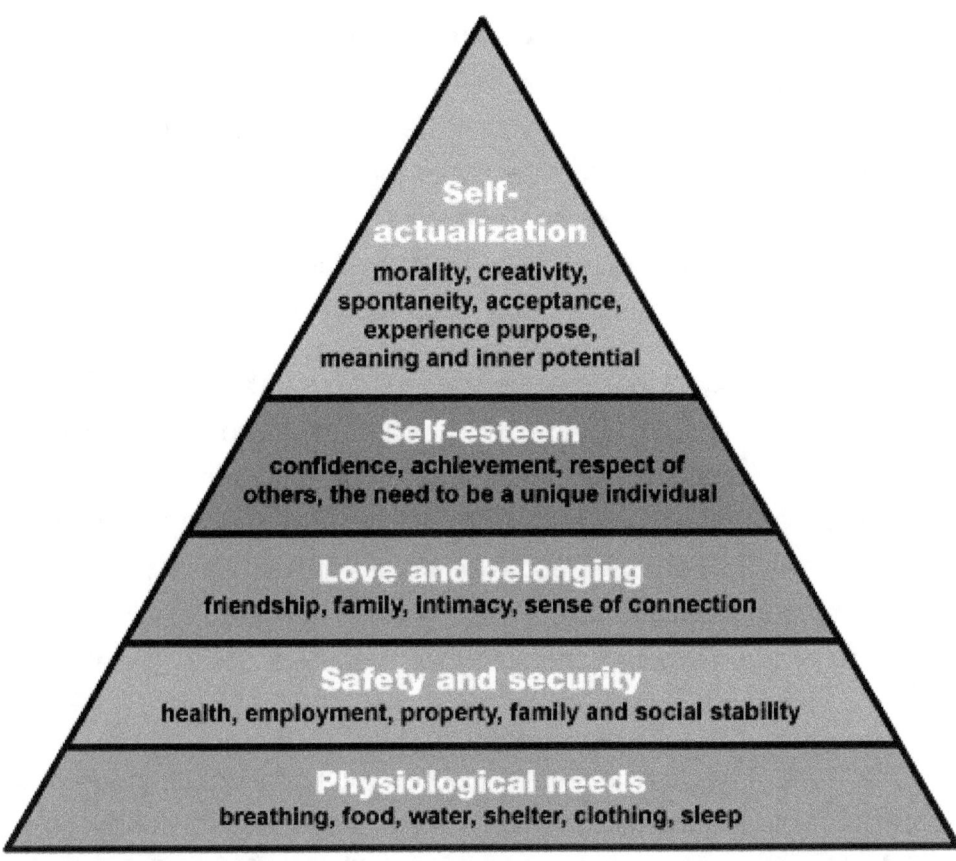

Maslow's hierarchy of needs is portrayed in the shape of a pyramid, with the largest and most fundamental levels of needs at the bottom, and the need for self-actualization at the top.

Maslow's focus in discussing the hierarchy was to identify the basic types of motivations, and the order in which they generally progress as lower needs are reasonably well met. Some who are still trying to meet their physiological needs will not be an advocate for your company because they will be focused on their own basic needs. At the second level—safety and security—you will find people who write for a living, such as professional journalists, bloggers, magazine writers, and editors. In social media, most word of mouth is actually written, not spoken, and the people in these professions have good clout and definitely need to be included in your circle of friends for conversations. So, read what they write, find where they write, join their conversation with your true comments, follow them on Twitter, get the RSS feed for their blog, become their Facebook fan, and if you find something nice that can be shared with your friends, then do so.

Love and belonging are the needs that will generate the real advocates for your brand—people who are in love with your brand and feel a sense of connection. These may or may not be your current customers, so always keep your eyes open for such people as they might be someone you met or helped at any time in life. For example, one handyman company told me that they found their advocates from people with whom they shared their tips about fixing things in their houses, not just their customers. They have all those testimonials on their website now.

The self-esteem hierarchy represents people who might not be in love with your brand but are willing participants in the conversation about the brand and looking for recognition and association with your brand. So, create an environment where they are recognized among peers. These people need to feel that they belong to a community or are marching towards some higher goal. Praise them on your site (maybe links to their personal blogs or writing), mingle with them, and create a feeling of a common cause with them. Foursquare.com does this pretty well, they have mayors for their destinations, and having the most check-ins gives a person that title.

Self-actualization is the final level of psychological development—the level where the individual is realizing his greatest potential in the area of his strongest desire. Self-actualized people are achievers and accomplished individuals. They already have a name for themselves and influence in their communities. Their talking about a brand gives it credibility and appeal to others, but you have to create an awesome, spectacular, or remarkable conversation for them to talk about it.

I would like to make a couple of points here:

The strategy does not have to focus on a particular hierarchy level.

Anything that triggers something at the top will definitely trickle down to other levels, but the opposite might not always be true. For example, creating badges and contests for your community advocates might not always lead to a story written by top marketing guru or influencer, but it definitely helps your community members to work towards achieving that status. On the other hand, having a top influencer who loves your brand regularly interacting in your community will definitely help trigger further conversations.

> *TIP:* Now you know the different sets of people who can trigger conversations for you, so plan to engage them based on their needs.

Now that you have seen these different sets of motivation levels, your job becomes different. Now the focus of the organization is toward *creating conversations,* not *initiating conversations.* Wow, it looks pretty simple and straightforward, but the task is quite challenging. That's why as a leader you have to do things differently and orient your team to develop content that creates conversations among your target market.

> *TIP*: Your customers are your best marketing team. Ask any Apple product owner!!

So as an owner, your job has changed. Instead of spending time creating marketing material, sending press releases, printing mailers, and then using the traditional channels, give your customers something to talk about and watch what happens. Your community will do the marketing for you, and you will build a community of advocates and friends who are part of your family. Those are the two things that are most critical to success. Just like any other relationship, your efforts are focused on nurturing the relationship and making them feel special for their contributions and socializing/meeting with them to keep them surprised at all times. *Do the unexpected for your community advocates and they will do the unexpected for you!!!*

Ask yourself who you trust the most when you want to go on a trip: friends, colleagues, your doctor, your pharmacist, your boss, an online expert, travel websites? The answer to that question will demonstrate how community advocates can benefit your business.

You have seen it all over but didn't recognize it: TV commercials showing users sharing their real experiences (remember Progressive commercials?), direct mailers publishing quotes from customers, radio commercials having real people talk about real experiences…it's been in front of your eyes all the time, and you didn't recognize it. It happens to all of us.

The principles of WOM remain very simple—it is just like talking to your consumers face to face. Keep it conversational, be authentic, be open, and give them a quick response.

TIP: Make a community of friends who are going to be part of your family. Now, you have support of both a family and friends.

THE ART AND SCIENCE OF WORD OF MOUTH

The art is how to deliver the conversation, which depends on each individual. Some basic guidelines can definitely help guide the conversation in the right direction. By the way, these are also very useful in any face-to-face conversation:

- *Understand that conversation begins with being a good listener.* Hey, *listen, not hear,* your customers, employees, colleagues, and I would even venture to say everyone—yes, even your wife and kids! We marketers have always made our way by being great talkers, and our ability to talk has been a sure sign of success for us. Well, now, let's try to change that, and keep ourselves in listening mode when we're having conversations with anyone. We'll be able to get a totally different perspective, and that triggers good long conversations and relationships.

- *Show genuine interest in others.* Dale Carnegie once said, "It's much easier to become interested in others than it is to convince them to be interested in you." This holds true even in online conversations. If you show that you're giving full attention to the other person's problem or issue, half the battle is won. The other half is how you respond to it.

- *Never flatly disagree or show hostility.* Even though at times this can be very tempting, it is best not to bluntly disagree with your customers. The customers are sometimes agitated (as happens to all of us), and they are looking for someone to listen to them and help them resolve the issue. In instances where the issue can't be immediately resolved or there isn't enough information, then let them know you will find out and get back to them.

- *Praise in public.* If someone is doing a good job, acknowledge that in public by saying simple things, such as "Thanks for your kind words" or "Thanks for your retweet." In the words of Brutus from

Shakespeare's *Julius Caesar,* "But when I tell him he hates flatterers, He says he does, being then most flattered." I would not say that we need to flatter people unnecessarily, as it starts looking artificial at some point, but acknowledge the people who are promoting your word of mouth.

- *Stay and close on a positive note.* Conversations over the phone with your customers or your responses to online comments or email should leave both parties with a positive spirit (most of the time). Using positive words during the conversation and ending on a positive note will leave a good impression and likely bring them back for more!

- *Recognize that you will receive some negative comments and be prepared to handle them.* Chapter 8 includes specific advice on dealing with the negative.

CHAPTER 2: IS SOCIAL MEDIA WORD OF MOUTH?

A recent survey done by CMOsurvey.org (http://bit.ly/cmosurvey2011) says that social media is word-of-mouth marketing, although the survey results reveal that most large marketers spend about 5.6% of their budget on social media! These business leaders feel particularly bullish about this marketing channel. Survey participants predicted that their social media spending could rise to 18.1% of the marketing budget by 2016. Ads produced $3.15 billion in revenue in 2011 for Facebook.

This projection highlights the fact that companies are waking up to the possibilities of social media, so you should cash in before the others do. But before doing so, you need to understand what social media actually is.

Professor Andreas Kaplan, a noted authority on marketing, has described social media as "a group of Internet-based applications that build on the ideological and technological foundations of Web 2.0 and that allows the creation and exchange of user-generated content." The key phrase in this definition is "user-generated content." But, isn't word of mouth user-generated, too?

This leads us to the big question: is social media word of mouth? Consider the following facts of social media and you might be able to get a clear picture.

AN INTERACTIVE PLATFORM

The various forms of social media bring together a huge number of people from all over the globe via the Internet. Blogs, forums, social networking sites, social tagging, video sharing, and microblogging are the arms of the ever-growing entity that is social media. People might come together on a particular website for any number of reasons, but once there they might soon start discussing your product. Wondering how and why? Consider this: Most social media sites are a mode of interacting with real people.

So, many people who by nature are reticent feel free to share their opinions about various products and services with others who are online. They may be thousands of miles apart, but the Internet, being an open democratic forum, allows unbridled exchange of ideas and information.

And the number of people, who might be discussing your product or service at any time, using social media tools, is simply mind boggling! According to the survey conducted by PewInternet (http://bit.ly/whyusesm):

- Two-thirds of online adults (66%) use social media platforms such as Facebook, Twitter, MySpace, or LinkedIn.

- Connecting with family members and friends (both new and old) is a primary consideration in their adoption of social media tools.

The results reported here are based on a national telephone survey of 2,277 adults conducted April 26–May 22, 2011. 1,522 interviews were conducted by landline phone, and 755 interviews were conducted by cell phone.

SOCIAL MEDIA IS MARKETING

The basic 4Ps of marketing: *Product, Price, Promotion, and Place*, and the 3 Cs: *Company, Competition, and Customers*, still hold true in the social world that influences your "marketing mix." This "mix" is not a magic powder that can spice up your business, but a well-thought-out plan!

It is basically the breakup of what you are offering to potential customers. Social media can be called a tool for promotions. But then, you are not doing anything on your own! The only other promotional tool that is powerful yet unintended is word of mouth. 90% of word of mouth happens offline, that is, via face-to-face conversations between people. So, social media cannot replace conventional marketing tools but can definitely boost their effectiveness.

14

This is what many major corporations of the world have found out. They did not need to swoop into the realm of social media marketing because they have bottomless funds for engaging in mainstream marketing tactics. But they have, because they know the power of word of mouth. So, companies such as,

- Coke (http://www.coca-colaconversations.com/), Southwest (http://www.blogsouthwest.com/), Disney Parks (http://disneyparks.disney.go.com/blog/), and Dell (http://en.community.dell.com/dell-blogs/direct2dell/b/direct2dell/default.aspx) use blogs.

- Adobe (http://www.delicious.com/popular/adobe) and Kodak (http://www.stumbleupon.com/discover/kodak/) use social bookmarking .

- Dell (http://www.ideastorm.com/) and Starbucks™ (http://www.mystarbucksidea.force.com/) use public opinion via voting and idea-contribution sites.

- IBM (https://www.ibm.com/developerworks/mydeveloperworks) and Intel (http://embedded.communities.intel.com/community/en, http://communities.intel.com/community/openportit, http://communities.intel.com/community/tech) use communities to interact with their target markets.

The list could be endless, but the bottom line is that these companies have tried and benefited by integrating social media in their marketing plan. You can, too!

SOCIAL MEDIA IS LISTENING

The best marketer does not do different things, but does things differently. In order to be the best marketer, you need to interact with customers via social media platforms and allow them to give their unadulterated views on your product or service. You need not react to these opinions in words. Instead, you can act on them, to improve your offering. So the customer gets to know that you have listened to him or her.

In today's age when many companies are literally shoving their products towards customers, if you can buck the trend and listen to your customers first, you can go many notches ahead of your competitors in the customer's mind. After all, you have to give respect to get respect.

If you keep tabs of the type of word of mouth your products or services are getting on various social networking sites and blogs, you will find that it reflects various emotions such as satisfaction, dissatisfaction, or even indifference. You can get new ideas and complaints on which you can work. You should take constructive criticism that comes your way as an opportunity to improve and not as something to feel bad about. After all, even criticism indicates a high degree of interest from your customers.

> *TIP:* Follow the C.L.E.A.R philosophy: Connect, Listen, Engage, Advocate, and Repeat.

Take it as a challenge to understand what the customers want and how that can make your product better. Listening to customers is a surefire way of getting them involved deeply with your product. So do not miss that opportunity.

> *TIP:* When you are listening, be ready for all types of comments: positive, negative, neutral, and mixed, as well as questions.

SOCIAL MEDIA IS COMMUNICATION

Social media can also be your best communication tool in the digital age. The job done by traditional press releases can be done equally well, if not better, by social media releases. In your attempt to reach out to all stakeholders (employees, customers, shareholders, creditors) social media can be the best mouthpiece.

This is what websites such as prweb.com, pitchengine.com, prnewswire.com, businesswire.com and marketwire.com help you do.

Pitchengine.com is every small business owner's dream. This site helps you prepare and share social media releases with all your contacts and everyone else on the web. And it's free too. Imagine the opportunities this site could open up for your business. Your press release remains online for a period of thirty days, thus allowing readers from all over the world to have access to the information.

Pitchengine helps you take conventional press releases to the next level and can be the perfect tool to start a viral marketing campaign. Move over email attachments and word documents because Twitter pitches and Facebook summaries are here to replace you, thanks to pitchengine.com. It's little wonder that they have clients such as IBM, Toshiba, PespiCo, and Xerox using their services. And they are only some of the more recognizable names among the 14,000 plus companies of various sizes who have benefited from social media releases via this site.

To top it off, pitchengine.com also offers small business owners the chance to own and operate a customized social media newsroom. For as little as $550 a year, you can:

- archive every release that you make,

- choose a headline font color that is in sync with your company logo or brand name, and

- give interested visitors a chance to follow you on Twitter, Facebook, Flickr, YouTube, and many more sites.

Seriously, this is the best you can get without hoping for miracles to happen! But if you think these guys are good, what about prweb.com? *Prweb.com* is a site which offers online news release submission and distribution services. For a small business owner like you, they can:

- attract new customers,

- provide you huge publicity,

- drive sales and profits through the roof , and

- increase the hourly traffic to your website.

In fact, prweb.com is *the* largest online news distribution network. They have more than 40,000 clients ranging from small entrepreneurships to mammoth multinational companies, all of them looking for global exposure via social media. Of the different packages they offer their clients (which, at press time, start from a mere $80 per news release), the Social Media Visibility package is the most popular. It helps your news release

- reach industry specific websites and blogs,

- be shared on Twitter, and

18

- get measured for effectiveness by tracking viewer responses.

You also get a chance to promote yourself via Google Adwords. So, along with spreading your message across social media, you can expect prweb.com to:

- *Help you reach millions* of prospective customers. Unlike email marketing, you are no longer restricted to just the few hundred names on your mailing list.

- *Help you attract the eyeballs* with news releases that are virtual sales brochures.

- *Make sure your news is exposed to thousands* of journalists and bloggers who are scouring the Internet for story ideas.

- *Make your information viral.* The sooner it is shared on social media, the faster it can become a big story on the Internet.

- *Teach you how to create the best news releases*, avoid common mistakes, and get the most out of every dollar you spend.

> *TIP:* Not just for external communications, social tools are very useful for employee communications as well.

SOCIAL MEDIA IS RECRUITING

Hal Thomas got a cushy job with BFG Communications with a single tweet, a message posted on Twitter, the microblogging site. His 140-character tweet was a creative bit of work that spoke volumes about how much he wanted the job. He linked to a modified picture, showing him on the cover of *Wired* magazine, with a made-up cover story that described how he had taken BFG to the top of social media business. His message also contained a direct link to his blog.

The recipient of the message, Sloane Kelley, content director at BFG, later said that Hal had displayed all the qualities required for that particular post, most important being his social-media-savvy nature. The proof of the pudding lies in the eating, as they say, and Hal had provided a sumptuous meal via his Twitter message!

Though this might seem like an isolated incident, the fact is that more and more employers all over the world are using social media to recruit the right people. Creativity in presenting applications via Facebook, Twitter, or other sites is being considered a masterstroke.

Some sites are being preferred more than others, mainly due to the demographic profile of their members. Sites such as MySpace and Second Life, which have a young user-base, are usually ignored in favor of sites such as Facebook and LinkedIn, where the user profile is just right for recruitment.

Employers, particularly those from the IT sector, find fresh or soon-to-be graduates and post-graduates on these sites very easily. Most people on the verge of completing formal education maintain profiles on the web 2.0 sites. The trends are the same all over the world.

The second annual Cisco Connected World Technology Report (http://bit.ly/ciscoreport), which surveyed more than 2,800 college students and young professionals in 14 countries, was commissioned to assess the challenges that companies face as they strive to balance employee and business needs amid increasing network demands, mobility capabilities, and security risks.

IMPACT ON JOB CHOICE AND SALARY

The study revealed that one in three college students and young employees under the age of 30 (33%) said that they would prioritize social media freedom, device flexibility, and work mobility over salary in accepting a job offer.

Mobile networking, device flexibility, and the blending of personal and work lifestyles are key components of a work environment and culture that are increasingly important in determining which companies will land the next wave of industry talent.

More than two of five college students (40%) and young employees (45%) said they would accept a lower-paying job that had more flexibility with regard to device choice, social media access, and mobility than a higher-paying job with less flexibility.

This works because most job offers are a result of referrals, and social media sites involve many such bonds between people that encourage them to help each other out when needed.

LinkedIn has all 500 of the Fortune 500 companies as members. There are a total of 130,000 recruiters from about 130 different industries. These recruiters:

- *Stay in touch* with former colleagues who they feel can be a part of their team once again in the future.

- *Actively search for candidates by using keywords* aimed at locating the right candidates. Candidates on their part, try to maintain keyword-rich profiles, which can highlight their qualifications and experience.

- *Search for candidates based on "recommendation notes,"* which is a specific feature of LinkedIn.

- *Ask their present employees to recommend names* from their networks on LinkedIn.

- *Post jobs on LinkedIn*, which allows them to do that for a fee.

According to LinkedIn, they combine "job listings, candidate search, trusted referrals and the power of networks to give you results."

Facebook is not left behind with BranchOut™ (http://branchout.com/) and BeKnown™ (http://www.beknown.com/landing), recruiting applications getting more popular day by day. Don't leave Facebook out if you are planning to find a new job or a new candidate.

So, even though the debate about its correctness rages on, companies are looking at a potential employee's public profile before hiring. This might be in addition to studying their resume/curriculum vitae and interviewing them. They know that a candidate will always put their best foot forward with these conventional pre-employment discussions, but looking into their profiles allows the knowledge of who they are in reality. There are aspersions being cast over the ethics of looking into people's closets and hunting for skeletons, but this practice continues to grow every day.

SOCIAL MEDIA IS CHEAP

One of the main reasons why social media is a boon for businesses is the fact that it is so cheap. What other media can give you so much exposure and other benefits for so little? You can get all the above-discussed benefits for very little investment. But at the end of the day it is up to you to make the most of this virtually free box of goodies.

The low cost is a double-edged sword as people tend to dive into it too soon without a plan and think they can come out of it without damage because it's free. You can fail miserably without proper planning. *The real investment is in time and resources.*

SOCIAL MEDIA IS INNOVATION

More and more companies are using social media as a tool for innovating and upgrading products and processes. They have realized that customers can be the best critics for their products and services and using their ideas can be really beneficial in the long run. Some of the companies are:

- *Dell Computers,* which launched Idea Storm (http://www.ideastorm.com/) as a way to talk to their customers directly. The Dell business model involves the act of bypassing the middlemen and selling custom-made PCs to the customers. This website helps them strengthen their bonds with the customers, who are their lifeblood. Via the website, customers and Dell have brainstorming sessions. New ideas and suggestions are actively sought and deliberated upon. Nearly 400 new ideas have already been implemented in new Dell products.

- *Starbucks,* which started the website http://www.mystarbucksidea.com with the intent of connecting with their customers and shaping the company's future with their assistance. Via this website, members (all that is required to become a member is to sign up) can post new product and service ideas, vote on other people's ideas, discuss the pros and cons of various ideas, and also see which ideas have been implemented so far. The ideas involve products, experience (ambience, payment, ordering, etc), and involvement (community building and social responsibility). Talk about getting more stars for your bucks!

- *Fidelity Labs*, which encourages co-development of applications over the Internet by using http://www.fidelitylabs.com/ as a platform. It encourages anyone interested to create and share new web tools. Customers can also try out their latest applications, which are usually in the testing phase. This gives customers a chance to make their suggestions known to Fidelity before the main product is launched. Wells Fargo also has a similar site.

So, you can see how much social media is being used to create product and service offerings, which can provide effective solutions for users.

SOCIAL MEDIA IS CUSTOMER SERVICE

You may know quite well that a business cannot survive without proper customer service. Gone are the days when there was no interaction between the seller and the customer post purchase. Nowadays, one purchase creates an everlasting relationship between you and your customer. To make this relationship deeper, companies are flocking to various social media sites.

The reason is quite simple. The rules of the game have changed, whether you like it or not. Very recently, Hewlett Packard, the IT giant, committed a customer service gaffe by charging a customer $1099 for repairing a machine that was still under warranty. Some years back not many people would have known of this, but today, the entire world knows! The aggrieved customer posted this issue on Crunchgear.com, a web 2.0 tech forum, and HP received a blot on its rather clean image. It takes only one bad incident to tarnish goodwill built over years.

As HP's experience shows, and many other brands have found, social media has changed the way you should think about customer service. An isolated incident can have huge ramifications due to the fact that customers are connected to each other like never before.

Companies such as Zappos (http://twitter.com/#!/zappos_service),
Wells Fargo (http://twitter.com/ask_wellsfargo),
Bank of America (http://twitter.com/BofA_Help),
Delta Airlines (http://twitter.com/#!/@DeltaAssist) and many more, have started offering customer service using social platforms. Their customers are made to feel that they are never alone.

TIP: Customer service has become really real-time with social media tools. Consumer expectations are changing, and 24-48 hour email turnaround time will not be acceptable in the coming times. Have a plan to use this platform for your customer service issues.

SOCIAL MEDIA IN ALL FUNCTIONS

You may get it by now that the possibilities of social media are endless. If you choose to adopt social media, you can imbibe it into every aspect of your business, to the extent that you want. But standing at the threshold of a new decade, you must understand that the way forward is joining and creating relationships with your existing, previous, or potential customers.

We have already discussed a lot. But the essence of it all is the fact that social media can and will slowly be the primary link between businesses and their stakeholders. If you divide society into producers and consumers, you will find that there cannot be any such divide. Every individual is a producer as well as a consumer, in one way or the other. Social media is the platform where all come together to attain the common goal of improvement, regardless of geographic and other boundaries.

Social media tools can be used in all functions of the business so it all depends how you would want to use them.

Culture Change—If you go to your marketing person and say you want to increase sales using social media, and his response is, "Yes, let's do it, create a Facebook page, Twitter account, and LinkedIn profile, and start getting followers using direct mailers, banner ads, a full-blown campaign...," hold back. There is something missing in the picture. The power of social media is the ability to let the community talk about you, and your role is to be creative about generating those ideas. Marketing's role has changed from creating content to be consumed by customers to creating content that will be shared by their customers using social tools.

The same rules apply as if you are having a face-to-face conversation with your customers:

a) listen (not hear);

b) take interest;

c) know your topic;

d) communicate honestly, clearly, and openly;

e) stay positive;

f) don't be a know-it-all and redirect as necessary; and

g) finally, close the loop.

Using this approach will get you to the point where you are not chiming in all conversations and your other fans (not just customers) will chime in for your brand, so your team doesn't have to do all the work.

So, there is very little to stop you from using social media for business growth. Profiles on Facebook, Orkut, LinkedIn, and Twitter are all you need to get started. You can, of course, take this forward and create a full-blown e-marketing campaign with mailers, banner ads, and the whole works, but then you might miss out on the essence of social media. The fact that social media helps you engage humans all over the world in discussion and debate over your products and services is what makes it so special. No fanfare, no hullabaloo, just the viral effect of word of mouth. Get your customers to speak for you—every marketer's utopia!!

CHAPTER 3: SOCIAL MEDIA TOOLS

When the activity on the Internet increased and people started getting hooked on it, many sociologists said that the Internet will make people asocial. However, this did not happen. People are still socializing. Today's world has become web-social. You want to make friends? You want to build professional relationships? You wish to share photographs or videos? You want to increase your knowledge or you want to let people know how you are feeling about burning or ignored issues? All these can be done on the social media tools available on the Internet.

SOCIAL NETWORKING WEBSITES

Social networking websites are the most popular of all the social media tools. Participating in these sites provides a fantastic method of getting in touch with new, old, and long-forgotten friends. You can get in touch with your friends from school, colleges, universities, and workplaces or with your childhood neighbors or your lost love staying in any corner of the world. There is a long list of social networking sites. However, the one most talked about these days is Facebook.

FACEBOOK

Facebook was launched on February 2004 and reached 1 million users within the first ten months of operation. The latest statistics from Facebook (http://bit.ly/facebooklatestinfo) indicate the site had more than 845 million active users by the end of December 2011, 50% of their active users log on to Facebook in any given day, the average user has 130 friends, and, collectively, people spend more than 700 billion minutes per month on Facebook.

In Facebook, a user can create a profile. There is a Wall in which your contacts can post messages for you, which works well for simple message exchanges. You can also share your photos with your contacts. With a Poke feature, your friends can virtually keep poking you whenever they want. The poke is a feature of Facebook whose sole purpose is to attract the attention of another user. The only thing that happens when you poke someone is that this person receives a poke alert on his or her home page. Users can poke only a confirmed friend, someone in a shared network, or a friend of a friend.

The basic features of Facebook are a person's Home page and Profile. The Home page includes News Feed, a personalized feed of the user's friend's updates. The Profile displays the information about the individual that he or she has chosen to share, including interests, education and work background, and contact information. Facebook also has some core applications—Photos, Events, Videos, Groups, and Pages—that let people connect and share with each other. Additionally, members can interact with one another through Chat, Birthday Reminders, Personal Messages, Wall Posts, Pokes, Status Updates, or Facebook Places.

Using the gifts feature, you can buy a virtual gift for your girlfriend for $1 and attach a personalized message to her as well. If you tend to forget her birthday, Facebook will give you a birthday reminder.

Facebook offers the option of creating groups. A person can create a group or can join an existing group. A group can be created out of classmates, college friends, university alums, industry, or a common hobby. You can join a fishing group or a gardening group. You may find a group of your classmates who are trying to connect to the whole class in school or college. I'm a member of the group "I Use my Cell Phone to See in the Dark" as this is exactly what I do. This is the group of people who cannot live without a cell phone.

There are some funny groups like "When I was your age, Pluto was a Planet," "People Who Always Have To Spell Their Names For Other People," "Unlike 99.99% of the Facebook population, I was born in the 70s," "Flipping My Pillow Over to Get To The Cold Side," and many more (*Source*: http://www.facebook.com/pages/). Try joining any such groups and you will get to meet people with many humorous stories.

Brands can create Facebook pages for promoting their companies. You can go to those pages and "Like" a particular brand. Usually their Facebook vanity URLs include their brand names, for example, Nationwide Insurance has its Facebook page as https://www.facebook.com/nationwide, Bestica has its Facebook page as https://www.facebook.com/bestica, Coca Cola's Facebook page is https://www.facebook.com/cocacola.

Facebook has a statistics package called Insights. It is meant for pages users and social ad users to get relevant data regarding ad performance statistics, fans' demography, and trends in the web market. This is a useful application developed for business owners who use Facebook to promote their brands and launch new products.

Perhaps Facebook Polls is the right application for you. It has the multimedia support and an edge due to millions of Facebook users.

Facebook also allows you to link your Twitter profile to your personal or Fan page, so you can share views and news with your fans in Facebook and followers in Twitter at the same time. You can install apps that allow you to share only selective tweets at http://apps.facebook.com/selectivetwitter/.

Facebook also includes interesting apps, and you can check them out at http://www.facebook.com/apps.

TIP: Create a custom Facebook page using the Static HTML app: http://apps.facebook.com/static_html_plus.

TIP: If you are selling a product or service, a profile in Facebook will really help you improve your business prospects. You need to join a group whose interest can be somewhat related to business. For example, if you are selling dog-related products, join a group that loves dogs.

LINKEDIN

LinkedIn is meant for professional networking with colleagues, superiors, and subordinates of your professional life and has over 60 million users (*Source*: http://en.wikipedia.org/wiki/LinkedIn).

LinkedIn is based on the concept of multi-tiered connections called contacts. One person connects to some of his professional colleagues and seniors (first degree connection), who in turn are connected to their colleagues, seniors (second degree connection), and so on. Thus the network of people whom you know professionally also increases. You don't have to wonder if the information in someone's profile is accurate, you can trust it because of your mutual connections, and you can be introduced through a mutually trusted contact.

This site helps the professional find a job through his links and helps an employer find a suitable employee through his network of professionals. The LinkedIn Jobs page (http://www.linkedin.com/jobs) has all the openings for jobs in the United States posted by participants, and you can search for a suitable one for you. Employers can have the vacancies listed to find prospective candidates. Hence, if you are looking for a job or for an employee, you ought to be there or you will be left behind.

LinkedIn also offers lots of apps that can be used in your LinkedIn profile (http://www.linkedin.com/static?key=application_directory).

> *TIP:* Join Groups on LinkedIn related to your professional interest. If you are a designer, then join design-related groups. You will share and learn a lot by interacting with people who have similar interests.

GOOGLE+

This section wouldn't be complete if I don't talk about Google+, Google's latest venture in social networking. This time Google might have hit the nail on the head, and Google+ could become a ubiquitous social option in the coming months. Here is an overview of its features:

Circles: Groups of people you share content with. You can create new circles but some circles are provided by default: Friends, Family, Acquaintances, and Following. Posting a status update in Google+ is not like sending a Tweet or updating Facebook. The core functions of an update are the same as Facebook—photos, links, video and location, but the difference is that Google+ gives you an option to decide which circles your update is posted to—from individual groups to all circles, to extended circles, or to just a single person. You create your own "Circles of Trust."

Streams: Streams give you the option to see updates from people in all your circles or you can choose to see updates from only one circle. Under streams, there are two other options below your circles—Incoming and Notifications. Incoming will show you messages that have been sent by people outside your circles. Notifications will show you when people in your circles post an update or comment on something you have posted or commented on, or if someone adds you to their circles.

> *TIP*: An interesting feature in the Streams is that conversations will surface back to the top when subsequent comments are made on them. Google developer Jean-Baptiste Queru calls it "Bumping."

Sparks: This feature helps you find content on the web that interests you. Google+ does provide some "Featured Interests" like Cycling, Fashion, Movies, Recipes, and others. You can share articles found in Sparks with a Share button on the bottom of every article.

Hangouts: This group video chat feature can have up to 10 members and best of all it's FREE! You can wave goodbye to VoIP companies that charge for this feature.

MICROBLOGGING

It is usually said, "Great ideas are often spoken in few words." I wonder if that was in the minds of people who created the wave called microblogging. In today's world, everyone is hard-pressed for time. Often, it is easier to write a message as small as 140 characters for the people who wish to hear from you rather than writing in length. Twitter, Jaiku, Plurk, and Yammer are some popular microblogging sites.

TWITTER

With 75 million users, Twitter is currently the leader in the field of microblogging. It is a message service and a discussion forum where microblogs are called tweets. It's been used extensively for personal users telling their friends about what they're going to wear to the upcoming party as well as business users providing for customer service and brand promotion. With more than 200 million registered accounts, Twitter doesn't need anything else said.

Twitter helps in creating groups of friends and followers and in group tweeting. While writing a tweet, there is an auto complete feature that helps you write faster. If you are introducing a web link in your tweet, it is taken as one character and gets hyperlinked to give a neat look to your tweet.

Twitter also gives you an opportunity to display your name along with your tweet. It helps in finding people who are interested in your messages. If you are following too many people and your twitter feed is overloaded, you can easily mark the favorite ones.

Twitter provides a "Lists" feature that enables users to put their followers or people they follow in different categories.

Another feature called "Contributors" helps you give a personal touch to the communication between a business and an individual. The user name of the contributors is appended to the tweet by-line. In this manner, customers get to know the person behind the brand. Now, brands need to add an agency or their employees as a contributor and he/she can tweet under the brand name. Imagine how empowered employees and agencies can handle various kinds of conversations at the same time!

TIP: The service http://bit.ly automatically shortens long URLs to save some character space on Twitter.

TIP: All brands need to check out the "Twitter for Business" page: http://business.twitter.com/.

JAIKU

Jaiku is a microblogging site owned by Google. With the same 140-character limit, you can create an activity stream and follow friends.

There is a list of contacts for communication and you can find and add more friends, share updates, see their availability, calendar of activity, and leisure. It has a special functionality called threaded messaging and threaded comments which makes it more suitable for web, SMS, and IM.

You have the option to create your own channels. Channels allow multiple people to contribute in one single stream.

The number of users is fewer than Twitter. If you are one of those who would like good features but feel suffocated in cluttered places, this is a good option for you.

PLURK

Plurk lets you send short instant messages or text messages called plurks to your followers. It helps the users send messages and updates to all or some of your friends. For example, you can tell your office friends on Plurk that you are not well, hence not in the office, while informing your friends that you are on a one-week vacation to Hawaii. Once you are back, you can share your images and videos on Plurk as well.

Plurk supports group conversation among friends and facilitates the use of emoticons to express your mood. It also helps in translation of these messages to the local language through its own translation website.

YAMMER

Yammer is a microblogging site with a difference. It focuses on businesses instead of individuals. Hence people from the same email domain can join the site. Profiles of the users who have left the company are deleted. The rest of the features are the same as in any other microblogging site: it lets you send and receive updates, tag content, and select followers.

You can create public and private groups within the network. You can send files and images as attachments. It helps in customization of network color and logo. It also has the feature of social bookmarking.

TIP: For customer service, you should be a part of the microblogging tool that is most popular even if you don't like cluttered places.

VIDEO SHARING

Who can deny the powerful role of videos in getting attention on the Internet? Websites with only text seem to be boring to today's netizens. Videos have become an easy way to attract readers. And these videos have enhanced effectiveness with a pinch of humor. Video acts as a tension reliever and an entertainer, not just a source of socializing.

According to comScore's "2012 U.S. Digital Future Focus Report" released in February 2012, more than 100 million Americans watched online video content on an average day to close out 2011, representing a *43% increase* versus a year ago. People share videos from their professional life and personal life—especially kids. Companies are finding it an inexpensive yet effective method of communicating to the target audience as well as increasing their brand recognition.

YOUTUBE

This is the most famous video-sharing site, used exhaustively for sharing personal as well as business-related videos. Some interesting YouTube statistics:

- Sixty hours of video are uploaded every minute, or one hour of video is uploaded to YouTube every second.

- Over 4 billion videos are viewed a day.

- Over 800 million unique users visit YouTube each month.

- Over 3 billion hours of video are watched each month on YouTube.

- More video is uploaded to YouTube in one month than the 3 major US television networks created in 60 years.

- Seventy percentn of YouTube traffic comes from outside the US.

- YouTube is localized in 39 countries and across 54 languages.

- In 2011, YouTube had more than 1 trillion views or almost 140 views for every person on Earth.

(Source: http://www.youtube.com/t/press_statistics)

You can upload videos up to 2GB in file size; hence, the video quality of your professionally captured video remains intact. YouTube has a feature called Insight that tells you the sources of how the users found your video. This tells you how to make your video more popular by increasing the traffic to your video. You can use Annotations to add text or links to other videos in any of your videos.

If you do not have a sufficient number of videos on any topic, you can use the YouTube feature of Favorite Related Videos and create a list of related videos. It also has editing tools with which you can add captions or subtitles to cater to the international community or a hearing disabled person.

If you have an iPhone, you can shoot a video and directly upload it to YouTube. This feature is extremely helpful for human rights organizations or organizations dealing with disaster relief. People who are part of any nonprofit organization can use the pop-up sliders to advertise for their organization and to ask for donations when someone is watching their video.

If you do not wish to watch a long video, you can skip directly to the time by mentioning the time that you wish to skip. Enter #t=1m3sec after the URL of the video and the video will start from the point of time indicated, in this example, one minute and three seconds. With the Autoshare feature in your YouTube account, your video, your list of favorites, and feedback are automatically transferred to your other accounts, like Facebook, Twitter, and Google Reader.

Here are some ways you can use YouTube for your business:

- Sharing Videos (Automatic sharing on Facebook and Twitter from under the "Settings")

- YouTube Insight

- Video Promotion (Very similar to PPC concept)

- Uploading HD Video

- Commenting on videos from your industry

- Favoriting Videos

- Creating Playlists

TIP: Download the YouTube creator playbook: http://bit.ly/youtubeplaybook.

VIDDLER

Viddler is another interactive site for uploading, sharing, and making groups around videos. This video-hosting service is accompanied with a very good blog. It helps in creating private groups and is supported by detailed analytics for a business user. One hundred million served and counting!!

The most identifiable feature of Viddler is the customizable Vidget (or widget) that makes the sharing of a playlist of videos much easier. The videos can then be embedded in various ways. Also it seems much faster than YouTube. A business user can add a logo or brand to the video for the purpose of advertising.

UTTERLI

Utterli is hybrid social media. As the name suggests, it is for those who want the world to hear them. This service helps you upload multiple types of files. You can broadcast your cooking tips or your new poem through an audio or video file. You can upload text with a picture as well. Utterli provides the option of recording, hence you can record your voice as you "utter" and upload it. This site even gives an option of recording and uploading a live web chat. Utterli enables uploading a file from a mobile as well; hence, it is easier to use this site.

BREAK.COM

Break Media was founded in 2004 and is headquartered in Los Angeles, CA. Its principal investor is Lionsgate Entertainment.

It is a leading creator, publisher, and distributor of digital entertainment content including video, editorial, and games. The company's properties include the largest humor site online—Break.com—as well as Made Man,

GameFront, HolyTaco, ScreenJunkies, CagePotato, AllLeftTurns, TuVez, and Chickipedia.

Break Media specializes in creating original videos that range from award-winning branded entertainment to celebrity-driven web shorts to viral one-offs. The Break Media Network represents hundreds of publishers as one of the largest video advertising networks online, reaching more than 125 million visitors each month.

Of course they have a Facebook app; you have to search for 'Break Media" under http://www.facebook.com/apps.

METACAFE

This site is solely dedicated to showcasing the best short-form videos from the world of movies, video games, TV, music, and sports—programmed for today's young male entertainment drivers.

The Metacafe magic comes from the fact that they deliver:

- More exclusive, original, and curated premium video content than any other entertainment site

- Twelve million unique monthly viewers (40 million worldwide!)

- Innovative custom creative solutions that deeply integrate brands into the entertainment experience

The Facebook app allows you to share and keep track of your favorite movie trailers, video games, music videos, and other premium entertainment you watch on their website. Adding Metacafe to your Facebook Timeline is really easy. Just click the new "Add to Timeline" button when you watch a video, and they will do the rest for you.

LIVE STREAMING

Live streaming is one step ahead of videos. It is a delivery method in which audio and video are received in real time. It is targeted or presented to an end user and is delivered by a streaming provider. Media such as radio or TV distributed over the telecommunication network fall in the category of live streaming. Live streaming can be on your computer, mobile device, or TV.

Live streaming helps in conducting webinars and webcasts, live streaming of videos and speeches, and holding a real time event, so this is useful for individuals as well as businesses. Some of the most popular live streaming sites include Ustream, Qik, Hulu, Vimeo, and Justin.tv.

USTREAM

If you are a member of Ustream, all you need to make a live broadcast is an Internet connection and a webcam. Users need to just enter the title of the program, description, and uploaded artwork. Once they click start, the program starts streaming. The users can tweet the URLs or send them in an email. If you are a savvy user, you can create picture-in-picture and other visual overlays as well. You can track your favorite shows. Users who are watching a video stream can live chat with others participating in the stream. It is used not just for live display of personal events but also in teacher-free learning and distance education.

QIK

Qik is another live streaming option with features that enable members to use their profiles in other social networking sites. Based on technology perfect for a mobile video platform, it provides fast, reliable, and excellent quality video. It is simple to use and secure. Hence this is being used by event and news broadcasters, as well as for giving a glimpse of magical moments of personal life like a child's first step.

Qik's goal is to offer the most flexible solution so that individuals can focus on capturing great moments knowing they'll be able to:

- Share with anyone—across handsets, platforms, carriers, and networks

- From wherever—reliable transmissions over 3G, 4G or wifi networks

- View whenever—show videos LIVE or anytime later

- Capture forever—automatically preserve precious and once-in-a-lifetime moments

In January 2011, Qik was acquired by Skype.

TIP: You can successfully use live streaming for discussions related to the latest news items in politics, science, or commerce in your educational institution.

PHOTOS

There has been a lot of activity around video on the Internet. This does not mean that the still photos have lost their sheen. There are several sites that host your stills capturing those magical moments. Indeed photography is an amazing way of staying in touch.

FLICKR

Flickr is perhaps the most well-known online photo-management service. I have an account with Flickr, and I really like its features for cropping and editing a photograph and for organizing photos around a central theme, like a picnic or a mountaineering trip. You can share your photos with the entire world or just your close friends. You can create posters, calendars, cards, and photo albums using your photographs.

PHOTOBUCKET

Photobucket not only allows the sharing of photos but also videos. However, it is more popular among people who wish to display their photographs online. If you have an account with Photobucket, you can send the link of your photographs to your family and friends and they can view them without creating an account. It helps in creating a group album where a group of your college friends can contribute all the college photographs that any of you clicked 10 years back in college. You can edit and fix photographs in frames and also create a slideshow. There is an online gift store that helps you get your photograph printed in mugs, cards, calendars, luggage tags, jigsaw puzzles, stickers, and other items.

SNAPFISH

Snapfish is another good option for online photo-sharing. It has user-friendly software and has made assembling photos online a much easier task. It offers photo books in various sizes and binding options. It facilitates high resolution uploads and representation of photos in a themed template. You can get these pictures printed as well. As in Flickr, you can share your login ID and password to allow your loved ones to see your photographs.

PINTEREST

The latest social network getting a lot of buzz is Pinterest. Simply put, Pinterest is a social network that allows users to store, share, and get to know new interests by "pinning." You can upload images from your computer or pin things you find on the web using the Pinterest bookmarklet, pin it button, or just a URL.

Pinterest's goal is to connect everyone in the world through the things they find interesting.

Get yourself familiar with some Pinterest jargon:

- Pin: A pin is an image added to Pinterest.

- Pinboard: A set of pins.

- Pinning: The act of adding a pin.

- Repin: Resharing or reposting someone else's pin.

- Pin It Button: A button that gets installed in your browser and lets you grab an image from any website and add it to one of your pinboards.

- Pinner: A user of Pinterest.

Compete (http://www.compete.com) reported that unique visitors to Pinterest.com increased by 155% in just one month, from December 2011 to January 2012. So, have a plan for this network if you want to drive more traffic to your site URL.

According to BlogHer's annual study on women and social media, when asked whether they trusted different social media sources, 81 percent of women representing the general US population said they trusted blogs and Pinterest, while 67 percent said they trusted Facebook and 73 percent said they trusted Twitter. (The questions were asked of those who indicated that they used each of the social media services.)

BLOGS

A blog or a weblog is a website that has commentary, news, or articles around a central idea displayed in a reverse chronological order. It is generally maintained by a single person and can also have graphics and videos. Blogs can be personal or maintained by organizations and business corporations. They can be written in any of the different languages of the world and on any subject, such as travel, politics, fashion, education, or projects. They can be created on laptops, mobile phones, iPods, or cameras. They have become a wonderful way of communicating your point of view. People can read through the topics and provide their feedback on it. It also helps in developing a community around a thought or a mission. There are search engines, like Technorati, Bloglines, and Blogscope, designed especially for searching blogs on a particular topic. Technorati tracks close to 1.3 million blogs for its ranking (http://technorati.com/blogs/directory/). So, if you have something in mind that you want to share with the world and earn money as well, it's time to start writing on your own blog!!

TYPEPAD

Typepad is a blog-hosting site for businesses and professional bloggers. A person need not have technical knowledge to create a blog in Typepad. It has features like built-in spam control, an intuitive editor, and a variety of design templates that are rich in multimedia effects. It also has mobile blogging capabilities.

WORDPRESS.COM VERSUS WORDPRESS.ORG

WordPress is free blogging software available on the Internet. It is available in two forms—WordPress.com and WordPress.org.

WordPress.com hosts your blog for free and has space and customization constraints. You do not need to have technical knowledge to use WordPress.com for blogging; however, you are not allowed to run advertisements.

WordPress.org provides the blogging software for free but does not host your blog; you need to pay for a domain name and hosting your blog on the Internet. There are no space or customization constrains; however, you need to have technical knowledge to be able to use this. You can monetize your blog through WordPress.org by running advertisements and installing various themes and plugins.

BLOGGER.COM

This is another popular blogging site run by Google. It is user friendly and allows you to add photos and videos. It has some advanced features like the ability to post a blog through your mobile device and group blogging. You can also use third party applications that are permitted under the code of Blogger.com. You can write a blog in any of 41 languages to reach to your target audience.

TIP: If you are not confident of your technical skills, do not try them on your blog. You might mess up things and hence lose all the data that you had placed on your blog.

EVENTS

When event management and planning were not done through the Internet, event organizers had hardly realized that their reach can be much greater. Earlier they had a targeted list of people who were attracted through hard core marketing and professional promoters. All this involved much more cost than is now necessary. Why? Social media tools have event search and promotion sites that give much better results at hardly any cost. Even organizers can use these tools to promote their events themselves. They can advertise on the Internet mainly through word of mouth publicity. They communicate to the audience directly and make a note of their feedback, which helps them in improving their event and obtain maximum customer satisfaction. In any conference, several deals get signed by the members and new relationships get built. Events search and promotion sites are highly beneficial in this as well. Some of the most popular sites for events are Yahoo Events, Eventful, and Facebook Events, all of which let you announce, find, review, and discuss the upcoming events in the town.

FACEBOOK EVENTS

Facebook Events lets you create an event where you need to give the name and description of the event, its time and place, and the name of the event creator or the host. You can share the events with others who tell you whether they will attend or not. You can also add the date and time to your personal calendar so that you do not have to remember them and are able to plan in advance. You can upload your pictures and share your views with other participants of the event.

Facebook Events has an additional feature where you can keep the event open or restricted so you get to know which events you can attend. The host can also mention the type of event, whether it is a party, conference, sport event, trip, or exhibition.

YAHOO EVENTS

Other than the basic features of adding and promoting an event, Yahoo Events has a strong event finder that lets you search events by city, state, country, and ZIP code. It also has a service called Yahoo Event Pride, which helps you find the details of several historic events.

EVENTFUL

This is another useful site for searching, tracking, and sharing information about the most happening and not-so-happening events in any city across the world. This, too, has the option of keeping an event private or public through an option provided in the calendar.

The feature My Eventful (http://eventful.com/my) is the watch-list of events that any of the users can create before confirming their participation. The users can also have a list of their favorites and import their profiles of Last.fm and iTunes libraries to mark favorite performers.

A new feature is Eventful Demand, where people can create a demand for the kind of event that they want to participate in or the kind of performance that they wish to see. They can create a campaign around that demand and encourage others to join it. Depending on how strong the campaign is, the event managers can hold an event and invite the campaigners and others as well. Now you know what you need to do if you wish to see a performance in our city.

SOCIAL BOOKMARKING

Social bookmarking is the method by which we bookmark the information available on the Web. Many times we read an article on the Web and email the link to a friend or a family member. By sending that link, you are actually bookmarking that article. The article is getting bookmarked on the Web and not on your own Web browser. There are several websites like Digg, Delicious, StumbleUpon, and Reddit that help you in bookmarking an article, a news items on politics, or information about sports or a technological development. If you and your friends are interested in cars or mobile phones, any one of you can bookmark the related news and all others will be able to read it.

With the over-abundance of information on the Internet, finding something relevant through the search engines is like searching for a pearl in the ocean. Instead of searching through the search engines, now you can simply go to the social bookmarking sites, go through the links in the area of your choice, see the votes that the article has received and you will be able to know what to read. By sending a link of a website, you have actually helped in making that page popular and search engines will pick it more often than it was doing earlier.

Digg is a user-friendly site that lets you bookmark, vote, and comment on the news and social news write-ups. It is most popular among all social bookmarking sites and gives you tags on a variety of topics. You can cast a positive or a negative vote, depending on whether you liked or disliked an article.

StumbleUpon has a more personalized service and displays pages for you based on the ratings given by your friends on your network. It allows posting comments in the manner of discussion. The positive and negative votes are cast through thumbs up and thumbs down. It has successfully applied the knowledge of user preference for targeted advertising of various sites.

TIP: StumbleUpon now drives over 50% of all social referral traffic to US websites beating even Facebook, as per report from Stat Counter http://www.stumbleupon.com/su/2Mr2vv/gs.statcounter.com/#social_media-US-monthly-200903-201108.

Delicious is another popular site for sharing, storing, and finding bookmarked items on the web. It has features like tagrolls, linkrolls, network badges, and RSS feeds that can be used to show bookmarks on blogs. It also has the most popular and recent pages listed under Hotlist.

Reddit is extremely easy to use, and the focus is not limited to mainstream news headlines. Just like Digg, Reddit allows you to cast a negative vote on something that you did not like. Hence, it is not always a safe option for searching for something relevant.

TIP: Social bookmarking is extremely useful in marketing of your blog. If you wish to popularize your blog, you need to ensure that it has more and more votes and tags on the various Social Bookmarking sites.

COMMUNITIES

The social media tool called Community Builders (http://www.joomlapolis.com/) helps you create a community around any central theme. This tool has a combination of synchronous features like chat, instant messaging and web conferencing for real time communication and asynchronous features like email list and web-based discussion boards for communicating at one's convenience. Some of the best-known community builders are Joomla, Ning, Kickapps, Igloo, Drupal, Socilago, and Stribe.

Joomla—The community-builder suite of Joomla has key features like more user profile fields (hence the user needs to give more details about himself before joining the community), user lists and connection paths between them, image uploading capability, PMs, newsletter, forums and galleries. It lets you search for a user using multiple criteria and gives the developer of the community full control on the core fields. However, it requires you to pay for starting a community on CBuilder or for becoming a member.

Ning is another popular community builder that lets you customize the visual appearance of your community on the site and the fields of the member profiles, so you can create your social network easily. The developer of the community, however, has some degree of control over the features of the community. For the community, there is a central page for blogging and social networking tools to be used by each member of the community. If you opt for the paid option of Ning membership, you will not have to see the ads posted by Ning on your community page, which are visible in the free membership option.

Kickapps—If you are developing a community in Kickapps, you will be able to get some advanced applications to customize its features, and you can also integrate it with your own website. The style and theme builder helps in matching the theme of your community with that of your website. It has the usual features like message boards, instant messaging, profiles, and guest books. It also has widgets to make your community popular and include more and more members. The membership payment condition is the same as with Ning.

Igloo is a free social-collaboration platform. After joining a community on Igloo, members can publish blogs, wiki pages, and newsletters. They can conduct polls, discussions, and events within their network or outside it. Igloo also allows you to customize the features to a certain extent.

Drupal—The creators of Drupal were inspired by Ning and wanted to make it a strong competitor. It is free and highly scalable and expandable. It is easy for a geek to create a network on this platform. However, this is not as easy for a non-technical person to use.

White Label Communities—The white label community or white label social network is a new form of community builder meant for business enterprises. There is always a demand for more effective networking tools for businesses that can enhance information exchange with a broader audience in the market. They also need to tap the internal knowledge base and improve on internal communication and information exchange. All this is required at the minimal cost. Hence the answer was white label communities.

There are several vendors for white label networking who offer community building platforms that can be fully customized and re-branded as per the needs of the enterprise. They require low investment and provide quick time to market. The building of a network is fast and effective, which leads to fast marketing of the product.

Mzinga facilitates the process of interaction of an organization with its customers, business partners, and employees in the same environment through connecting, collaborating, and communicating, allowing you to attain greater business values. The organization can have blogs from the head of the organization or its various departments. You can have a news and events section to give an update to everyone in the community of the organization. The core strengths of Mzinga are its administrative tools, which help in rapid scaling up of the community; comments feature; live chat; and message boards. Features like reporting and dashboards are extremely useful. However, it is weaker on the innovative side.

Jive Social Business Software (SBS) rightly boasts that it has 25% of the Fortune 100 companies as its clients. Its marketing and sales module includes features like customer relations management (CRM), enterprise class security, and strategic consulting. All this helps in getting you to hear what the customers of all generations across the globe are saying. The corporate communication and HR part helps in managing employees of various generations who are locally or globally placed and in measuring their individual efficiency. There are other modules, such as customer support, government, employee engagement, market engagement, and innovation, to give an overall social community building and communication solution. However, the client facing analytics tool needs to be enhanced.

Lithium has got an edge over others with the social CRM suite. It has shown proven results with greater scalability of the community and has efficient features like forums, chat, networking tools on demand, launching, and strategizing support. However, you are going to miss the social features like wikis, videos uploading, and management and widget solutions.

WIKIS

We have talked a lot about connecting to people and sharing knowledge and information. However, we also need the knowledge banks that we can read and refer to before sharing knowledge. To meet these requirements, we have the software tool called wikis, which allow easy creation and editing of interlinked pages using simple markup language. The encyclopedia created collaboratively by all users is called Wikipedia. Other popular wikis include Scholarpedia (for scholars in any area of expertise), Wikibooks, Wikiversity (for free learning communities), Wikihow (how-to manual), Wikianswers

(answers to the questions that you post), Everything2 (essays), Wikiquote, Wikisource, Wikitravel, LyricWiki (lyrics by album), and so on. The webpage of Wikipedia (http://en.wikipedia.org/wiki/List_of_wikis) has the list of wikis on various subjects. If you think there is a topic missing on which you can create a new wiki page, you should start the project right now.

Here we have talked about the most famous and promising tools in each category of social media tools. However, the list of such tools is ever-increasing, and so is the list of categories that they cater to. This long list of socializing tools has led to the need for websites like prweb.com and pitchengine.com, which analyze and distribute news regarding the social media. Thus, if you wish to take benefit of social media for your business, just keep hooked to sites like these.

CHAPTER 4: DON'T KNOW AND DON'T CARE ABOUT SOCIAL MEDIA

A lot of businesses aren't aware of the true potential of social media, and that's why they aren't able to realize its benefits. We will go over the different social media tools and platforms and see how they can be useful for your business.

BLOGS

Blogs are Internet journals written in a conversational tone and updated on a regular basis. Blog readers are people looking to gain information along with engaging in conversations; they are usually more patient than users of other social platforms. Blog readers can also be really loyal customers.

What better way to reach out to your customers, present and prospective, than a blog? Here are some reasons why you should seriously think of having your own blog:

Convert Monologue to Dialogue—A blog helps you create useful and insightful content on topics woven around your offering. But unlike a monologue, here you get comments the very minute you add new content online. So, you are actually providing people the fodder for a conversation!

Customer Insights—Unique and vital customer insight can be gained because once the conversation starts around a blog post, people are usually expressive enough to reveal their preferences, dislikes, and opinions.

Public Communications—A blog is truly a public form of communication because anyone using the Internet becomes your intended audience. You can reach out to a much broader audience using your blog and thus create a long-lasting following for your brand.

Search Engine Ranking and Optimization—Blogs also allow you to use every SEO trick in the book to make your site rank highly on Google and other search engines. The more dynamic the content on the blog, the higher it will show up on search engines.

Flaunt Your Personality—Your blog posts reflect your brand, and there is hardly a better way to reveal the company's true personality to your audience. So if you wish to showcase the human side of your brand, then here is the perfect chance!

Easy to Start and Maintain—Starting and maintaining a blog is easy and inexpensive. There are blog software companies that offer easy blogging tools for starters.

You Own It—A blog scores over other social media platforms because this one is completely under your control. So, you don't have to deal with sudden changes in policies, privacy, and other issues on other social media sites, which might not be aligned with your internal corporate policies.

FACEBOOK

Facebook began as a college networking site and has now become the world's most popular social network. Here you can have a profile, which speaks as much as you want it to. Facebook friends can leave messages on each other's wall and one can even unfriend someone, which is to stop being friends in Facebook lingo.

Facebook users, or at least those who are active, are usually outgoing people who want to make conversations and friends with the world. Some people use Facebook to generate business and career contacts, while others use it to remain in touch with a close group of friends. Here you can get to know about the very personal likes and dislikes of people.

It would be a cardinal sin to talk about social media without speaking about the benefits of being on Facebook. So, here goes:

The 800 Pound Gorilla of Social Networks—Facebook is the biggest social network today. With over 500 million users and counting, Facebook gives you true global outreach. Moreover, half of these users log in everyday, so the conversations will never stop!

Facebook Apps—There are more than 550,000 applications or "apps" on Facebook that allow you to link up with various other social networking platforms and also do a host of activities on Facebook.

Facebook Pages—Your Page displays your public profile that tells people about your business and products. These pages can be modified as and when you like and can be made really attractive, too.

Facebook Ads—Facebook also allows you to create demand for your products with relevant ads, which can be even your own homepage. You also get real-time reports about the performance of your ads.

Facebook Connect—This is another great iteration of the social platform that allows you to connect your Facebook profile with other websites. Seamlessly integrating your other social media presence with Facebook has never been easier. But very soon, it will be replaced by an improved version called Open Graph, which was announced in the recent F8 Facebook developers' conference.

Top Stories and Recent Stories—The Top Stories are things Facebook thinks you might be interested in based on your interaction in the past. The Recent Stories appear in reverse chronological order. You can curate top stories by clicking on the tabs at the corners of the updates. Stories can be tagged as Top Stories or removed from the Top Stories list.

You can also hide certain friends' updates all together and you can change the sort order between Top Stories and Recent Stories on your Facebook home page.

Subscribers—The functionality is very similar to the "Follow" button on Twitter. Subscribers will receive your public posts and will not be added as friends. You can have broader conversations about public topics and keep personal updates for friends. It is a great way to create more connections with people.

Timeline—Your personal profile page is now called Timeline. Facebook describes it as "All your stories, all your Apps, a new way to express who you are." It's also been described as your personal scrapbook. One good thing about this feature that you can "go back in time" to view your activity.

Smart Lists—Lists can be created that update automatically based on info you have in common with select friends, like a school, job, or city. These lists help keep track of posts by certain groups of people.

So, if you live in San Francisco, you'll have a list of all of your Facebook friends who live within 50 miles of San Francisco. You can change this distance to adjust the size of the list, or manually add or remove people from this list. This list updates automatically as your friends update their timelines.

You can also create custom lists to organize friends as you like. You choose who goes into these lists and what (if any) privacy restrictions apply. Note that your friends won't get notified when you add them to custom lists.

> *TIP:* Custom lists can be deleted whereas smart lists can only be hidden.

TWITTER

This blue bird of microblogging is here, there, and everywhere! Twitter allows users to post status messages in 140 characters or less. Most users are tech savvy because they use Twitter from cell phones and PDAs and can message on the go throughout the day. They are also hungry for news and never want to be too far away from the action. Twitter users are the go-getters of these times!

The major advantages of being on Twitter are:

Microblogging—The very act of microblogging allows you to post short and impactful messages, enough to trigger conversations and create awareness, about what's new.

Instant News—Twitter can be your very own news distribution platform. With the touch of a few buttons you can reach out to all your followers simultaneously.

Customer Service—Twitter can also help you reduce the outlay on customer service if you use it for keeping in touch with your customers, thus discovering and solving problems quickly.

Communication Channel—Twitter is a social channel that can easily transcend the problems of engagement, such as time and resources. Both you and your customers can use Twitter anywhere and anytime.

Marketing Contests—You want to run contests? Twitter can help you spread the word and also host some of them. Twitter polls are also a great way of feeling the customer pulse.

Promoting Online Content—By providing links within tweets, you can promote your website, blog, or news releases on Twitter.

Reputation Management—Twitter, being the microblogging pioneer, allows you to enhance your brand, and also, you can search for your brand name on https://twitter.com/#!/search-home to see real-time who is talking about you and also chime into any tweets that can affect your brand negatively. For example, https://twitter.com/#!/search/coke link gives you real-time results for anyone mentioning "coke" on Twitter. So, your presence of Twitter also helps reputation management.

Ease of Use—Twitter is very easy to use and nothing that needs a tutorial. You and your employees can learn the nuances quickly, too. Just chunk down your thoughts in 140 characters or less…maybe that might need a tutorial. ☺

LINKEDIN

A social network with a difference is LinkedIn. It would be fair to call it a professional network because more than 67 million users from 150 industries in the world are members. More and more professionals are joining this site to build networks, find clients, and search jobs. So your target audience on LinkedIn is a driven bunch who are likely serious about using social channels for attaining career goals. A no-nonsense approach can be expected from them.

Shares of LinkedIn opened on May 19 , 2011 at $83 on the New York Stock Exchange, up 84% from its initial public offering price of $45. By the end of the day, the stock had soared 109% to $94.25 making the net worth of LinkedIn at $8.9 billion. LinkedIn's current market capitalization is $8.44 billion which is still very close to the initial high it received on its opening.

So what's in it for you?

Job Hunting—Most obviously, the fact that you get to view the resumes of thousands of people for free and at your own pace is one of the advantages of being on LinkedIn. People are using this social platform for job hunting and finding the right candidates for their companies. This will only drive up the number of members using the business networking platform.

Networking with other Professionals—LinkedIn provides the ability to join Groups. You should look for groups related to your industry and join them to meet fellow professionals. Don't forget, you have to participate in the group discussions not just join the group. LinkedIn provides a platform for many professional groups, where people from several companies, sharing a common job profile, engage in discussions that may yield a great deal of information about your stature in the industry. If you follow these groups, you may also find about how you can improve as an employer.

Building Brand Equity—Your present employees, who are probably on LinkedIn, may also have good things to say about you as an employer to their contacts. This serves as a handy tool in making your company more attractive for applicants.

Use Recommendations Effectively—Let people you have worked with recommend you on LinkedIn, as all public information is like having online references.

Update Profile and Install Applications—You should complete your own profile and use applications to display other work that you have done. LinkedIn provides you with a list of applications that can be installed on your profile (http://learn.linkedin.com/apps/) that enables you to collaborate, get insights, and finally showcase your work to the largest professional network.

YOUTUBE

If pictures say a thousand words, then videos speak volumes! This is perhaps why YouTube, the video sharing network founded in 2005, gets over 3 billion video views a day!! Check for some other interesting stats on YouTube here: http://www.youtube.com/t/press_statistics. Users of this site are people who value video over other forms of message and understand the universality of this form of communication.

This video sharing site has some great benefits, such as:

Video Sharing—You have an opportunity to show your expertise and your core values, run a social media campaign, help people solve some problems, or share just about anything you want the world to know about you. Best of all, it's absolutely FREE!! You can also make a slideshow with background music about your business or a new product. All videos can be shared on other social media sites like Facebook and Twitter.

Search Engine Optimization—The power of viral video is enhanced by the fact that YouTube is owned by Google. Creative videos can easily find their way round the world before you know it. YouTube is also very search-engine friendly, so you don't have to bother about additional ways to improve your search engine rankings if you are present on YouTube.

Promoted Videos—The videos you post can be promoted so that they show up higher in the search results on YouTube. You can also customize your YouTube channel to reflect your brand.

> *TIP:* Have a good multimedia strategy on the kind of audio/video content that will be created, the frequency of creation, and the process of approval and ensure that posting videos on YouTube is part of that strategy. As you mature your multimedia strategy, YouTube can also be used to post timely video responses to your customers.

This was a brief look at the top social media platforms and once you start using them, you will surely unravel even more aspects that can help you take your business to the next level.

WHY DO YOU NEED TO CARE ABOUT SOCIAL MEDIA?

Look at it this way: conventional e-marketing can be used by everyone, but if you want to make the best use of the web, you have to use niche strategies that may not have the greatest oomph but that will create an incisive impact nonetheless. Social media is the resource (or bundle of resources) that helps you devise new and useful techniques to promote your business, to become more visible, and ultimately to create and retain customers.

Here are the chief reasons why social media is the weapon of choice for big and small businesses:

1. Most conversations happen offline, but online conversations are gaining more popularity and you can't risk ignoring them. Social channels give people the opportunity to discuss their experiences with your products and services. And you may not know this, but people really talk about your brand all the time!

Of course the conversations about you and your brand may be good, bad, or outright ugly, but constructive discussion between users creates what is known as *user-generated content or UGC*. UGC is sought after by people looking to make a purchasing decision based on what peers and other social media users have to say about your product or service. That is why you need to be present where the conversations are happening.

Unless you join the conversations, you're much less likely to feel the pulse of customers, both present and potential. Neither will you gain valuable customer insight for free or at very low tracking costs. A conventional survey for doing these two things will cost you thousands of dollars!

And if you need more reasons to join these conversations, then just look at the present users of social media. Your customers, employers, employees, and prospects are there, so shouldn't you care about interacting with them on their platform of choice?

2. With the availability of improved technology, customers expect more from companies. They know that the resources are there for you to give them a better experience, and if you don't engage with them through these channels, they might quickly switch over to competitors who do interact with them.

So, no longer is simple product delivery a safe way to ensure customer delight. Customers expect more, and you have to deliver. The problem resolution-time benchmark continues to shrink. Now it's almost zero, thanks to social media.

Because social media allows you to be in the midst of your customers 24x7, you must also be able to respond to their queries and solve their problems in real time. If your competitor is doing it, and you are not, then you have a problem!

Look at how some of the biggest names in business are doing it:

Virgin America, the airline company, is on Facebook. The Facebook page (https://www.facebook.com/VirginAmerica) allows customers to make flight queries and receive updates all time. These are elements you would associate with a conventional company website or perhaps a customer service phone-call. But by integrating them with social media, Virgin has taken customer service to a new level of involvement. *Delta Airlines* is also very active in social media and launched its Facebook and Twitter (*@DeltaAssist*) for customer service as well as to gather feedback from their travelers.

Most recently they have launched a Twitter handle in Spanish, *@DeltaAssist*_ES (https://twitter.com/deltaassist_ES). Customers can expect the following from Delta via Twitter:

- Answer questions about Delta policy and procedures.

- Assist with lost baggage.

- Rebook a canceled flight.

- Help customers affected by general service failures.

Best Buy, the consumer electronics retailer, has taken to Twitter big time. They are encouraging hundreds of their employees to join their "Twelpforce" for customer service and company promotions. This will enable employees from across departments to handle customer queries, problems, and complaints in as little time as you can imagine.

Even financial giant *Bank of America* is now on Twitter just to be closer to their customers. They use two tags, *@BofA_Help* and *@BofA_Careers*, to help people with customer service and job information. The motto of their social media campaign is "We are here to stay in touch and serve you better."

Domino's Pizza learned a lesson about customer management, which is simply that silence is not golden when someone is tainting your name. In 2009, Domino's faced a YouTube crisis caused by two of their employees defacing pizzas and sandwiches in a prank video made viral on YouTube. But Domino's has since used social media to its advantage to enhance their brand and customer service and launched a website PizzaTurnAround.com (http://www.pizzaturnaround.com/) to face their critics and reinvent their pizza from the crust up. Perhaps all others too have been forced to take notice of the crisis management aspect of customer service.

A similar lesson of how powerful social media is in terms of customer management was delivered to *Southwest Airlines* when they refused to allow a passenger, Kevin Smith, to fly. Throughout the interactions between Smith and the cabin crew, the influential actor and director kept his Twitter followers (1.85 million, no less!) updated. This incident caused such as global backlash that Southwest was forced to publicly apologize.

3. Another reason for being in social media is because the youth is here. Yes, these are your customers of tomorrow, if they're not already your customers of today, and they are hooked up to the Internet. Social media presence is an important part of their lives, almost a matter of peer respect and social esteem. Sites such as LinkedIn are also helping them develop their careers by building contacts within their own profession.

According to a recent report from the Nielsen Company, (http://blog.nielsen.com/nielsenwire/online_mobile/what-americans-do-online-social-media-and-games-dominate-activity/), *Americans are spending a quarter of their Internet time on Facebook or other social networking sites, while online video games have passed sending e-mail as the second most popular online activity.* So, you cannot afford to miss out on being where young people are spending their time, which is in online networks.

4. The fact that sites such as LinkedIn are the choice of professionals to engage in networking also presents a great opportunity for you. Instead of engaging in expensive recruitment processes, you can track profiles of suitable people on social media platforms and recruit them to meet your needs.

On the other hand, social media is also becoming an effective tool when you want to run background checks on future employees because social profiles often reveal what's underneath the professional demeanor of people. So this can help you weed out the people you feel may be hiding things or presenting a false self-image. In this way, recruitment via social media is a win-win for you!

5. Social media also helps you speak up and speak out about your business and who you are. For decades, companies have felt comfortable enough to create strong brands and let them speak. But now customers expect the "real" you to interact with them, instead of an impersonal logo or brand staring them in the face. The time has come to drop the corporate façade and mingle with your customers. Even if you cannot become one of them, you need to come out from behind your brand and be more transparent.

Your social media presence shows that you are "for real"—a company with people who are willing to interact and not just sell. You can also portray your honesty by sharing your core values with your customers and making them understand that whether they make one purchase or thousands, they are an indispensable part of your business.

It is also safe to say that social media is the new communication medium. According to recent reports (http://www.newspaperdeathwatch.com/), newspapers are stopping their printed versions to focus more on their online presence. News is read online and spreads faster through social channels. So, the change is here and it's called *social media*—caring about it and participating in it are imperative!

CHAPTER 5: I AM CONVINCED. HOW DO I START?

Now you're convinced that social media is here to stay and you need to get on the bandwagon. But at this very stage a grave mistake is waiting to happen on the part of the planners, especially if they go in with a traditional corporate approach toward using social media. So, when you, too, are ready to make social media a communication tool for your business, you need to make sure that you do not try to cram social media into the mold of conventional corporate messaging.

SOCIAL STRATEGY

The foundation for creating a successful social media strategy lies in aligning it with the enterprise-wide, long-term strategy of your organization. Of course, you can set the broad parameters for this conversation by clever use of social media releases. Simply start the conversation. The buzz is created on its own, but only if the discussion heads where you want it to, or else the big bang you planned may end up a small whimper.

Here is what closed loop strategy would look like:

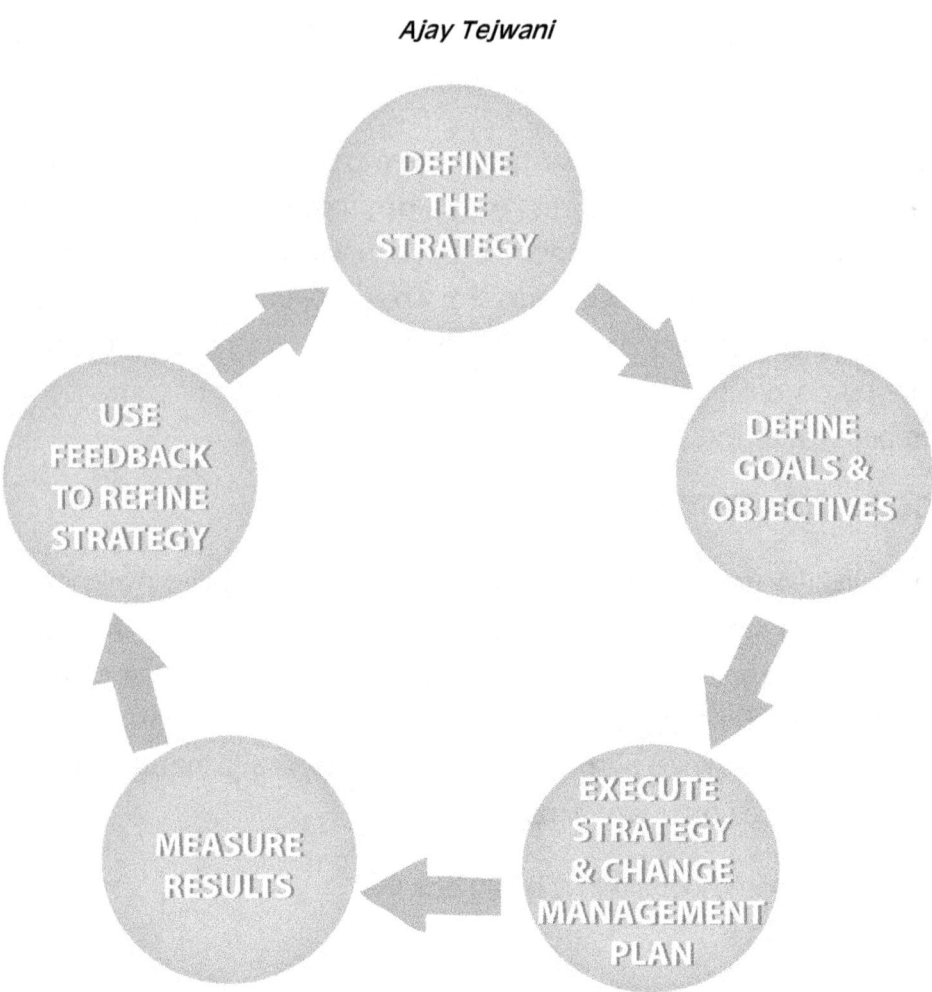

DEFINE STRATEGY

Strategy: a plan, method, or series of actions designed to achieve a specific goal or effect (Words myth Dictionary)

As management guru Michael Porter states, strategy is about differentiating yourself from your competitors and answering two basic questions (http://hbswk.hbs.edu/item/2165.html):

- Where to compete?

- How to compete?

TIP: Strategy is about making the right choices that will grow the organization in the long term.

Let's look at Coca Cola's strategy by looking at their mission, vision, and values (http://www.thecoca-colacompany.com/ourcompany/mission_vision_values.html):

Our Mission

Our Roadmap starts with our mission, which is enduring. It declares our purpose as a company and serves as the standard against which we weigh our actions and decisions.

To refresh the world...

To inspire moments of optimism and happiness...

To create value and make a difference.

Our Vision

Our vision serves as the framework for our Roadmap and guides every aspect of our business by describing what we need to accomplish in order to continue achieving sustainable, quality growth.

People: Be a great place to work where people are inspired to be the best they can be.

Portfolio: Bring to the world a portfolio of quality beverage brands that anticipate and satisfy people's desires and needs.

Partners: Nurture a winning network of customers and suppliers, together we create mutual, enduring value.

Planet: Be a responsible citizen that makes a difference by helping build and support sustainable communities.

Profit: Maximize long-term return to shareowners while being mindful of our overall responsibilities.

Productivity: Be a highly effective, lean and fast-moving organization.

Our Winning Culture

Our Winning Culture defines the attitudes and behaviors that will be required of us to make our 2020 Vision a reality.

Live Our Values

Our values serve as a compass for our actions and describe how we behave in the world.

Leadership: The courage to shape a better future

Collaboration: Leverage collective genius

Integrity: Be real

Accountability: If it is to be, it's up to me

Passion: Committed in heart and mind

Diversity: As inclusive as our brands

Quality: What we do, we do well

The strategy for small and medium-sized businesses mostly resides in the minds of the company founder or top management. It should be written down and shared with every employee so they can better understand the future of the company. This way the intended strategy by the management can be realized with help from employees and other stakeholders.

The company's mission statement defines its purpose, and in turn defines its enterprise strategy. The social strategy needs to be aligned with the enterprise strategy. For example, if you want to grow by 100% in the next three years, then social strategy needs to be geared toward getting more visibility with your customers and prospects. On the other hand, if your strategy is sustainment for the next few years, then use social channels to serve your customers better and streamline your backend processes. Use a social media plan that aligns with your strategy.

Any strategy needs to be based on internal factors—your company's culture, your employees and stakeholders—and external factors—political, economic, social, technological, environmental, and legal (P.E.S.T.E.L).

You will have to evaluate your company's strength, weaknesses, opportunities, and threats (SWOT analysis), maybe adjusting the current organizational structure to include social media as a team responsibility, not the job of just one person.

Hope this gives you an overview on how to develop a strategy for your organization.

DEFINE GOALS AND OBJECTIVES

Your goals serve as determinants of future courses of action and so must be rationalized to perfection. To make it easier for you to set some pretty sharp goals for your social media efforts, you can run them through the SMART-check. Each goal should be:

- *Specific*, which means that it should only relate to social media and be very well-defined for all to understand.

- *Measurable*, so that you can make periodic assessments that determine success or failure to achieve the goals.

- *Attainable* or practical enough to pursue, which means you need to involve all stakeholders and consider the resources you can employ before you decide whether a goal is attainable or not.

- *Relevant*, or how far the attainment of the goals can positively influence your business, which is important because social media holds different benefits for different businesses. Do a serious cost-benefit analysis to determine the degree of relevance a particular goal has for your long-term business growth.

- *Time-bound*, which means that you have deadlines for successful achievement of goals. You should allow enough time for pursuing goals, but also be prepared to modify or abandon goals that are simply not materializing even after a considerable amount of time has passed.

If your social media goals are SMART, chances are that you will be able to achieve them successfully.

Here are some goals that you can set during the initial phase of social media strategy:

Increasing brand awareness and recognition. NOT SO SMART

Ninety-five percent of our customers need to know about our entire service offerings by the end of 2011. SMART

We will get customer inputs for new product development. NOT SO SMART

At least 50% of our online community members will give us feedback for our new products within 6 months of launch. SMART

Improving internal communications and bringing about transparency in our business. NOT SO SMART

90% of employees should pass the social media training by the end of the year 2012. SMART

Improved search engine rankings. NOT SO SMART

Our company's website should be on page 1 of Bing, Yahoo, and Google search results for the following keywords: bamboo flooring, cork flooring, hardwood flooring. SMART

Our social media should be successful. NOT SO SMART

Our branded community should have 200 users by the end of year 2011. We will have an enterprise dashboard by the end of the year that shows our social media program success metrics and results. SMART

You may be pursuing one or more of these SMART goals, but once you get your hands into social media you will find that these goals are more closely tied to each other than you think. In fact, it is quite impossible to make progress with just one or two of these goals without making headway with the others.

Another important fact that you must understand is that all the above-mentioned goals are related to the most important objective of your social media efforts, which is to create engagement via dialogue. This alone helps you remain at the top of your (potential or current) customers' minds and lets you pursue all other goals. Thus, without a shade of doubt, this goal should be the crux of your social media strategy.

EXECUTE STRATEGY, INCLUDING CHANGE MANAGEMENT

You will need to create your change management plan—see the next chapter for more details. The next step is to allocate resources from various teams that will help you execute the plan. In an organization, teams that might be involved include the marketing team, the website management team, the legal team, the IT team, the communications team, the operations team, and perhaps others. Or in some small companies, one person could wear many of these hats.

The execution is where the rubber meets the road, and many companies fail or succeed based on their execution plan. Here are the things to keep in mind when creating your execution plan:

- Process Improvements

- Budgeting

- Resource Planning

- Marketing/Communications Planning

> *TIP*: A change management plan is crucial for successful execution. So ensure that all the relevant stakeholders, shareholders, and employees are on board for execution.

EMPLOYEES: YOUR FACE ON SOCIAL MEDIA

The key element in the execution plan is your employees. They help you achieve one of the key goals of social media marketing, that of humanizing your brand, by employee-customer interactions on various social media platforms. Having said this, however useful this may be, recent studies also show that the number of problems being caused by mishandling of social media by employees is on the rise.

For example, a recent study by Proofpoint (http://www.proofpoint.com/news-and-events/press-releases/proofpoint-survey-says-state-of-economy-leads-to-increased-data-loss-risk-for-large-companies?PressReleaseID=245) shows that out of several companies (that are avid users of social media) surveyed:

- Seventeen percent disciplined an employee violating blog policies, while 9% went as far as terminating the services of an employee for the same reason.

- Up to 17% of the companies are facing exposure incidents on sites such as Facebook and LinkedIn.

- Thirteen percent of companies surveyed have admitted to similar mishaps involving microblogging sites such as Twitter.

These bits of data point to the fact that while employees are into social media big time, many of them may not be doing it right. Thus, you need a framework to guide your employees on the correct usage of social media. In the absence of a proper structure, you cannot blame your employees for minor transgressions. However, if you have a set of well-defined guidelines in place, you can easily demarcate the rights and wrongs of social media usage for your employees to use as reference.

On January 25, 2012, NLRB (National Labor Relations Board) Acting General Counsel Lafe Solomon released a second report describing social media cases reviewed by his office. Download the report here: http://bit.ly/nlrbjan.

The report represents the Acting General Counsel's interpretation of the National Labor Relations Act as it applies to forms of communication that did not exist when the Act was written.

It is very crucial for your employees to have good knowledge of policies and procedures related to social media. Of course, your employees may already be on social media platforms and what they say online does not have to reflect the views of your company. Or does it? A workplace is usually a part of an individual's identity, except perhaps for the most intimate of conversations. In all other forums, blogs, chats, articles, etc., your employee does represent you in the eyes of your customers.

Therefore, you should make the rules of engagement pretty clear to every employee of your organization. Here are things you should consider while framing social media guidelines for employees:

How will it affect their productivity, if all are given freedom to participate in social media at work?

What level of restrictions are you looking at? You need to understand that completely curbing social media freedom can lead to lower employee morale and unwillingness to participate in your social media efforts.

How can you ensure that the guidelines are actually followed and not blatantly violated due to lack of understanding? For this, the best solution is to involve your employees, or at least the opinion leaders, in the process of creating guidelines and making them feel that a dictate is not being thrust upon them.

What are the penalties for violation you state in your social media guidelines? You must be able to enforce the penalty for a particular wrongdoing and make an example out of employees who abuse social media on purpose.

Social media guidelines are different for each company and reflect the company's general way of doing business. Nevertheless, you can go through the social media guidelines of companies such as Intel (http://www.intel.com/sites/sitewide/en_US/social-media.htm), Dell (http://content.dell.com/us/en/corp/d/press-releases/2006-11-09-00-policy.aspx), Wells Fargo (http://blog.wellsfargo.com/community-guidelines.html), and Best Buy (http://forums.bestbuy.com/t5/Welcome-News/Best-Buy-Social-Media-Policy/td-p/20492), to find out how the champions are doing it.

Finally, you should remember that if your employees are well educated about how the proper use of social media can lead to growth of the business and thus the betterment of their own careers, chances are much less likely that they'll misuse social media on purpose.

SOCIAL MEDIA MEASUREMENT

You will never know the true impact of your social media efforts without actually measuring the change brought about by using social media marketing. So, the question is, what can you measure in social media? This is a difficult question to answer when people usually think that the broader goal of social media is to build goodwill and nurture relationships with stakeholders. We will talk more about that in the subsequent chapter, but it is critical to measure success in social media and show the results to management, employees, and stakeholders.

USE THE FEEDBACK TO IMPROVE THE STRATEGY

MANAGING FEEDBACK

Your social media strategy should also answer one of the most important questions of all: how will you handle feedback? Feedback is the sum of what you get from your social media presence. You may find it in the form of response, criticism, praise, debate, argument, complaint, or even detached observations. However, the way you use feedback defines your success or failure with social media marketing.

If you accept the fact that your presence in various social media channels is because you want to be a better listener than your competitors and improve through whatever your customers have to say, then you should take all types of feedback in stride. You will find that you can broadly classify feedback into negative and positive.

Positive feedback is of course very encouraging and makes you feel that you have done a good job with your products and services. The fact that users have actually taken the effort to write a line or two of compliment for all to see speaks volumes about your success.

Positive feedback may also include queries regarding your product or service, which reflects interest from potential customers. It is critical to get back to these queries as soon as possible so that you can create a connection with the inquirer.

You may also receive mixed comments from users or fence-sitters, i.e. the first step in handling negative feedback is to determine the actual nature of it.

And, of course, you may receive feedback that is not positive. The following is a list of the different kinds of negative feedback you may receive:

Complaints: When a customer has a problem with your product or service, they lay it bare for all to know. It may be a specific and isolated problem, but it shows your business in poor light.

Critical analysis: This is perhaps the best type of negative feedback you can wish to receive. The aggrieved customer takes time out to give suggestions for improvement along with the actual problem. You can expect this from your loyal customers or those who expect high standards from your products. They will analyze the problem on their own and not just tear into you.

Personal/emotional attacks: You or your business has to cross someone very badly to receive this type of feedback. The problem is that you may not even know what the real issue underlying such a hostile response is. But, in most cases, there may be small but potentially serious issues for you to take care of.

Spam: These are off-hand comments about you or your brand, which are made by people paid by your competitors, to stain your reputation and hamper your social media progress. Other than being motivated by monetary incentives, some people may also tarnish your image in order to promote your competitor's product toward which they may have developed a great loyalty over time.

Once you have determined the type of negative feedback you have received, you should plan and deliver a suitable, timely response. The golden rule for responding to negative feedback of any type is to maintain a positive stance in your reaction. If you try to fight fire with fire, you may end up in a war of words with your customers that can take you miles away from the professional image you want to portray at all times.

Therefore, here are a few ways you should try to handle the different types of negative feedback:

Complaints: Provide an appropriate response, aimed at the specific problem or perhaps as a broader message if you feel that such problems may be faced by others too. If more than one person has the same complaint, you must answer with a public message. If a real problem (like a technical error or design glitch) exists, you must make your social media audience aware of the fact that steps are being taken to sort out the issue.

Critical analysis: Your response in this case should start off with a word of thanks for the suggestions, particularly if you do not plan to implement them any time soon, which will usually be the case. However, this may be a great way to increase customer loyalty and encourage your customers to keep providing rational feedback, especially for those who are of two minds about using your product or service. It is also important to communicate the facts to this group of people so that they can make up their minds and clear up any confusion they have.

Personal/emotional attack: The best way to placate a furious customer is to admit your fault, if there is any, for the issue that led to such a reaction in the first place. The customer might be venting and a little understanding will go a long way. The initial response can be along these lines: "You obviously feel our salesperson was rude to you. I understand you would be distressed about being treated disrespectfully. I will get to the bottom of this and get it straightened out for you."

After doing due diligence on the incident, you should clearly state how you plan to make up for the wrongdoing on your part. So, if you are offering a partial refund, be specific about this olive branch that you are extending towards an aggrieved customer.

Spam: If you fail to find logic behind a scathing attack on your product, service, or business policies, you should simply ignore it as spam. In fact, you should delete such comments, entries, or posts, which are simply meant to draw you into a fight. If the spam messages keep recurring, respond to the general public only, saying that you have explored the issue but are unable to verify its veracity.

> *TIP:* No feedback is bad feedback. Every response from customers is an opportunity either to know your strengths or to improve on your weaknesses.

The key is to constantly learn and improve—here are a few pointers:

- *Ensure* that mistakes on social media are not repeated.

- *Share* successes, no matter how small, with your employees.

- *Make changes* to your social media efforts gradually and involve all participants of your social media engine.

- *Keep* a keen eye on what the best in your industry are doing. If your competitor is doing better than you in the realm of social media marketing, there is no harm in taking a page out of their book.

You must also ensure that while riding high on the wave of social media success, you don't forget the necessary offline marketing strategies. They are the real breadwinners for your business, and ignoring them can be a serious oversight on your part!

The fact is that 90% of word of mouth is generated offline, so you cannot belittle the importance of conventional marketing activities to make sure that people are talking about you. Don't put all your eggs in the social media basket, or you may miss a bigger opportunity to make some serious profits!

Like radio ads using reviews from your site, email campaigns with actual testimonials from your customers prompt the audience for participation. Billboards and direct mailers should show your social media presence. Naked Pizza is using Twitter and QR codes in their print media and billboards to ensure that there they are able to leverage the power of traditional marketing to connect with their customers on social channels (http://bostinnovation.com/2011/02/25/naked-pizza-the-social-media-company-that-sells-pizza-opens-boston-location/).

Naked Pizza has received 8,000 investment inquiries in the past year and a half via online measures such as Twitter, where the owners post funny, food-industry-related tweets each day. The idea, the owners say, is not to drum up business using their feed. "The intent is more about starting a conversation in which like minds will engage," said co-owner Robbie Vitrano. "Some of those like minds, it turns out, are investors." (Source: http://on.wsj.com/wsjnp, August 2011)

If you accept that the use of social media is important for augmenting the scope of conventional marketing efforts as well as getting some great intangible benefits, you are on the right track. Having said this, also keep in mind that the importance of engaging customers via social media is growing at a rapid pace.

Finally, you are ready to step into the world of social media marketing. The world is going social, and you simply cannot keep your business aloof. Therefore, it is a good decision to explore the near uncharted realm of social media and maybe accrue benefits way beyond your expectations. Being a global citizen, you need to make sure that you reach out to one and all, without your talking points in tow.

TIP: If you want to succeed in social media, just stick to managing the parameters of conversation and not the conversation itself. It is easy and you can do it!

CHAPTER 6: SOCIAL MEDIA AND CHANGE MANAGEMENT

"Your success in life isn't based on your ability to simply change. It is based on your ability to change faster than your competition, customers and business." ~ Mark Sanborn

"Change is hard because people overestimate the value of what they have—and underestimate the value of what they may gain by giving that up." ~ James Belasco and Ralph Stayer, *Flight of the Buffalo* (1994)

"The true test of a leader is during changing times, so know your leaders by observing them in times of change." — Ajay Tejwani (2011)

You are always surrounded by change—large or small, for better or for worse. In business, as in life, managing change can define success or failure for you. As far as organizational changes are concerned, the sheer scale on which a new process or practice has to be introduced may make it appear like a Herculean task. In fact, the failure rate of all organizational initiatives that cause a high degree of transformation is a whopping 70%!
(http://ezinearticles.com/?Change-Management---3-Key-Reasons-For-the-Catastrophic-70%-Failure-Rate&id=2578395)

If you are ready to face the facts, you will agree that modern commerce cannot do without social media. The benefits of using this all-powerful tool for communications far outweigh the risks. But the million dollar question is: how can you incorporate the use of social media in your business without upsetting the applecart? The answer lies in change management. *Social Media is also a big change from the way we all have been doing business.*

WHY CHANGE MANAGEMENT?

Your employees are the primary stakeholders in your organization. Anything new that you try to implement affects them before it affects your customers and other stakeholders. The use of social media is no different. It is imperative that your executives buy into the idea and react positively towards its implementation. If they take this evolution as a bitter pill they must swallow, you can be assured that you will never get the mileage you can from social media. *People, in general, are not averse to change, but the primary cause of concern is communication about how the change will affect them.*

A change is nothing but a state of mind, but at an organizational level you are dealing with hundreds, perhaps thousands, of minds. The only way forward is that the alteration be accepted in unison, with employees at every level understanding the purpose behind the move.

This is why change management is critical for introducing social media into your organization, and perhaps the most important thing about change management is how you introduce it in your organization. After all, your organizational climate is unique, and you need to be very tactful in the way you present the idea of using social media to your employees.

CHANGE MANAGEMENT PROCESS

If you want to understand the entire process of successful change management, you should perhaps first look at the eight-step change process introduced by renowned business guru John Kotter in his book *Leading Change*. Using Kotter's principles, here are the steps to follow to effectively introduce social media in your business:

Step 1—*Create a sense of urgency*: If you can get the right momentum from the word go, it can be easy to implement a new idea such as social media. An honest and convincing dialogue with your employees may be one way of creating this urgency and getting them abuzz about the impending change.

Step 2—*Form a powerful coalition*: Although you may be able to manage the process of implementing social media by yourself, it is always good to share the responsibility of leading this change with key personnel of your organization. The influence can stem from experience, job title, or expertise. So, form a coalition of people with influence in your organization.

Step 3—*Create a vision for change*: The introduction of social media usage in your organization can create various ideas, suggestions, and perceptions in the minds of your employees. It is very important to have a common vision for all to understand, so that they can align their thought process accordingly. It is very important for your people to be able to visualize the future of the organization (specifically the benefits) after social media implementation.

Step 4—*Communicate for buy-ins*: Once you have the vision, you need to communicate the same across departments. Talk about your social media vision at every opportunity you get and encourage people to air their anxieties and queries openly, so that a dialogue centered on your vision can be started. This will facilitate better understanding and thus adherence to the vision.

Step 5—*Enable action and remove obstacles*: Once your employees are buying into the idea of social media implementation, you need to pave the way for a future course of action. This can be done by removing hindrances on the path of change. There may be people resisting change, and even your infrastructure and processes may be ill-equipped for it. So, you need to identify and address each of these problems before social media can become an integral part of your organization.

Step 6—*Create short term wins*: Often the long-term goals can only be achieved if broken up into smaller targets. And it is always a good idea to have feasible targets at the outset, so that their achievement can provide fuel for more effort from the entire organization. It is also necessary to win over critics or employees who challenge the idea of social media implementation.

Step 7—*Don't let up:* Use success at various stages of change implementation for setting future goals and as an index for further improvement. Many change management projects fail because of complacency and lack of continuous improvement. So, in order to make your social management implementation a complete success, you need to make sure that victory is not declared too early. Hire, promote, and develop employees who can implement the vision (change agents).

Step 8—*Incorporate changes into the culture:* Finally, if you want to keep reaping the benefits of change, you must make the new values and processes a part of your core organizational culture. This will make social media usage thrive and evolve in your organization because you will be working to make the practices better year after year.

These eight principles by Kotter are vital guidelines for implementing any sort of organizational change, including your social media implementation.

CHANGE AGENTS

Now that you are aware that in order to implement the use of social media in your organization smoothly, you must use effective change management, the next big question is how to begin. People working in the organization alter their mindsets and practices, and there are some who lead this process and help others embrace it. They are the change agents.

100

You can't make sure that every employee is viewing the use of social media in a positive light. But if change agents are present at every level of your organizational hierarchy, your job is bound to become easier. Needless to say, there is always the risk that your employees might dismiss your idea as a management whim. This is where a change agent can make a big difference.

He or she, being a part of the workforce, is not looked at by the other employees as a part of the management. So, your employees might just be more receptive to what one of their own has to say.

But then, how do you find change agents? There are two ways to locate these catalysts of change for your organization:

1) Look into your own workforce to find employees who have a positive approach to evolution and tend to look at long-term potential better than others.

2) You might even hire new employees to serve as change agents in your organization. A non-normative newcomer may be exactly what you need, because he or she does not have to indulge in unlearning.

Seek out potential change agents who exemplify the following characteristics: (Source: http://www.themanager.org/Strategy/change_agent.htm, Dagmar Recklies, October 2001)

- *Able to set realistic and well-defined goals.*

- *Sensitive to changes in management thought process and market conditions* and able to understand how such changes can affect the long-term goals of the project at hand.

- *Team-building abilities*, so that he or she can establish effective employee groups that have a clear idea of the responsibilities within them.

- *Superior networking skills,* so that they can lead the use of social media for communications inside and outside your organization.

- *Low level of responsiveness to an unstable working environment.* When your organization is in a state of flux, the change agents should continue to work efficiently so that others may follow their example.

- *Highly developed communication skills* to convey the need for change and also to convince co-workers about the long-term benefits of this change.

- *Interpersonal and motivational skills* to keep employee morale high.

- *High degree of initiative and innovation,* so that the change agent can lead by example and come up with solutions to problems without delay.

- *Selling skills*, which they have to display while trying to make the other employees buy into the idea of using social media. They must be able to project a positive image of the future so that your employees feel that you want to transform *with* and not *against* them.

Ideally, change agents should identify the opinion leaders and decision makers in your workforce and involve them to provide impetus to the initiative. You must, of course, train your team of change agents thoroughly so that they have no doubts about the benefits of using social media in your organization.

If you select the right change agents, you can use them in five different levels: (Source: http://www.corpchange.com/Resources/Articles/Areyouachangeleaderarticle.aspx)

Level 1: *Accepts the requirement for change and spreads the message* throughout your organization. Also defends the idea as and when necessary.

Level 2: *Takes initiative to implement change*, by targeting existing work habits and processes.

Level 3: *Helps translate the organizational vision into an achievable plan of action* for the workforce. Makes others see new opportunities in change.

Level 4: *Helps the organization through the transition phase* by creating a strategic practical course and balancing the present state with future objectives.

Level 5: *Champions the cause like no other.* Seeks to wipe out *what is* with a vision of *what can be.* These change agents can revolutionize your organization.

With a team of change agents working for the implementation of the use of social media, you can look forward to the change being set in motion.

The best change agents, in fact, are not the ones who stand alone. They are mostly looked up to by their co-workers because the change agents have gained respect by showing commitment and consistency over a long period of time. They don't mind if their jobs are on the line if they fail in their role as a change agent, but go ahead nonetheless and strive to complete the challenge facing them.

(http://www.businessweek.com/magazine/content/08_42/b4104096917161.htm).

> *TIP:* Remember that the job of a change agent is to influence change and not to manage it as a whole.

Finally, don't forget to motivate the change agents with incentives, which must be fulfilled once your change management is executed. You will be shocked to know that in a study of major change initiatives in Fortune 500 companies between 1995 and 2005, about 70% of executives who acted as change agents were left unrewarded, sidelined, and even fired (http://andyblumenthal.posterous.com/change-agents-poisoned-or-promoted). Make sure that you are not following this disturbing trend.

SOCIALIZE THE IDEA!

Your change agents are in place—now it's all about spreading the word. Your change agents will obviously have a major role to play here, so you must empower them with all necessary resources and authority to mobilize positive opinion about social media.

As discussed earlier, your objective is to make your employees understand the benefits of using social media rather than perceive it as a direct threat to their jobs. Here is an action plan for you to consider. (http://mashable.com/2009/12/28/social-media-business-strategy/)

1. *Outline the objectives of implementing the use of social media in your organization to one and all.* You can define social media objectives such as:

- *Increasing responsiveness* towards people and particularly your customers.

- *Obtaining feedback* more quickly than ever before from all stakeholders.

- *Bringing to the forefront the people* behind your corporate image. Social media can help the passionate employees of your organization who work tirelessly to achieve group goals get the recognition and respect they deserve from your customers. You can humanize your brand.

- *Creating greater global awareness* about your products, services, and company among consumers and future employees.

A well-defined set of objectives can help each employee select his or her priority when it comes to using social media. While your change agents should extol the benefits of social media at every opportunity they get, you should also look for CEO-level backing. If the CEO and senior management of your organization lend their full support to your initiative, your employees will find it much easier to see the logic behind using social media.

2. *Once your employees are comfortable with the reasons for using social media, gauge their capabilities of doing so.* You need to understand their level of knowledge about the usage and types of social media. Your change agents may help in assimilating this information and giving you a complete picture of your organization's social media readiness. If you find that the entire workforce is not yet familiar with social media, you may need to offer training.

Your company can use a similar set up for the dissemination of social media knowledge, ensuring that:

- fewer mistakes are made with the use of social media,

- mistakes made by an employee are not repeated by others, and

- the process of learning, and hence the integration of social media into your processes, can happen faster.

3. *Create an effective social media policy.* Here you might feel that it is not a wise idea to create arbitrary rules without knowing where the opportunities and threats lie. But you should know that most major organizations had a social media policy in place before they implemented the use of social channels. The social media policy developed by IBM (http://www.ibm.com/blogs/zz/en/guidelines.html) is a detailed example of a framework within which your employees are supposed to operate while using social media.

Try to treat your social media policy as a flexible framework that can always be modified in the future if you find better modes of using social media. Ideally your social media policy should have the following characteristics: (http://mashable.com/2009/06/02/social-media-policy-musts/)

- *Start by highlighting the takeaway,* or what your employees can do with social media. State in clear terms the immense possibilities that social media offers them to express their creativity and intellect as well as to ensure organizational and self- growth. Your policy should be a guide rather than a restrictive model.

- *Remind employees that they need to be responsible* about what they write. Some people can misinterpret the meaning of being expressive and, to be on the safe side, you should state clearly what the consequences of social media abuse can be.

- *Urge employees to keep the profile of your target audience in mind.* You are not only communicating with present customers but also courting prospective clients and employees. None of these groups should feel alienated because of your social media content.

- *Encourage the use of a neutral tone regarding controversial issues,* and ask employees to keep personal biases out of any comment they post. Your employees are representing the organizational image and not just themselves.

- *Your social media policy must clearly demarcate the type of information that cannot be shared with outsiders.* Classified information and internal affairs of the company should not be up for discussion on a public forum. Your trade secrets should remain yours!

- *Suggest to employees how to balance the use of social media with the other job responsibilities* they have. Unless specifically authorized, no employee should take time off from his or her main duties to use social media.

By now you must have a fair idea about how to pave the way for the introduction of social media into your organization by encouraging discussion, providing resources, and setting guidelines for the use of social media.

TIP: This is a very crucial step for employee empowerment and emphasis should be given to not only create, but also to clearly communicate the social media policy.

Spreading the word about the impending introduction of social media is vital for effective change management. The process starts with your change agents setting the wheels in motion and ends with you creating and providing the social media policy for your employees. This step can be time consuming but if you can successfully socialize the idea, you should be ready to start using social media without further ado.

SHARE SMALL SUCCESSES

Once you have started using social media, the real test begins! Of course you have already had to do much for getting things in place for the big change, but now is the time to reap the rewards for it. So, you should,

- Celebrate whatever little success you can achieve by using social media. Remember that you are taking baby steps forward and every step must be applauded to give your employees the encouragement to take the next one.

- Communicate to your employees and business contacts, such as vendors, any improvement metrics you might have at hand to prove that social media is working for you.

- Even if you have noticed an improvement in the organization culture and addition of new values and beliefs, it is as good as any quantifiable benefit. If the bonds of trust and mutual respect within your employees and also with the external stakeholders strengthen, it is reason for much joy. Don't let these soft benefits go unnoticed.

At the same time, you must try to improve the way in which social media is being used in your organization. For this, you should:

- *Encourage* suggestions from your employees, and try to create a best practices guide by incorporating useful ideas that have worked.

- *Identify* employees who are doing better than others in using social media, and encourage them to speak at team meetings to share their methods and tips.

- *Gauge* how your target audience is reacting to your social media releases, and solicit their suggestions as well.

- *Learn* lessons from mistakes, and make sure that they are not repeated again.

This will surely help social media transform your business for the better.

TIP: To ensure that your social media presence gives you the right results, provide more value to your users, followers, readers, and fans. (http://mashable.com/2009/06/02/social-media-policy-musts/). Providing value is also a necessary part of the change, as perceived by your present and future customers.

If you can manage change efficiently, social media can change your business. If you want to reach a new level of transparency in the way you do business, social media is the best solution. So, the choice is yours: manage change and soar on the wings of social media channels or keep following practices that might soon be labeled archaic and be left behind.

You should definitely take the first option—by now change management should not appear a Herculean task!

CHAPTER 7: THE NEXT STEPS

We've discussed in a previous chapter all that is happening in the social media sphere. Those of us who are running a business or working as an employee must remain active in social networks. Remember, we're not talking about increasing your personal social network. We're talking about commerce behind social media.

We've discussed various social media tools. It is also important to know that they can do wonders when integrated with your website – increasing the rank of your website, increasing customer satisfaction and, at the end, proving to be a good investment. Let's see what tools you can use on your website for the sake of your business.

SOCIAL MEDIA ON YOUR WEBSITE

RATINGS AND REVIEWS

For today's customer, there is no dearth of product options. If they do not like yours, they will simply move on. So it's extremely important to know what they are thinking about your product or service. Get to know what your customers like in a particular product and what is turning them off. This in turn will help your customers in decision making. According to Bazaarvoice (http://www.bazaarvoice.com/), the benefits include:

- *Increased sales*—Wehkamp, the largest merchant of The Netherlands, gets 80% of its sales from its website. The company saw a 20% increase in its average order value and 116% more sales conversion from those who read all the reviews of the product on their website. All this happened within just six months of launching a rating and review tool on their website.

- *Decreased return rate*—For premium pet food supplier PETCO, their product rate of return was 20.4% higher with customers who did not go through the product reviews than for those who did. Also, products with more than 50 reviews have far less rate of return than those that have less than five reviews. The significantly lowered return rate on products has resulted in considerable annual savings for PETCO.com.

- *Increased customer loyalty*—Bath and Body Works sells home fragrance and personal care products. *Repeat orders are 7% higher on products with reviews than those without ratings and reviews.* Also, people who posted their reviews on the site purchased 1.48 additional units on an average.

- *Drive product improvement*—The children's furniture company The Land of Nod chose to address a problem indicated in the product reviews of a particular product. When the improved product was launched, the company exchanged the old product of the reviewers with the improved one, free of charge. It came as a pleasant surprise for them. This was just the beginning of the product improvement stories at The Land of Nod and increasing brand loyalty that the company got from the reviewers.

Costco, which is one of the largest US retailers and the largest membership warehouse club, has a ratings and reviews section (http://reviews.costco.com/2070/24743/reviews.htm) for members to rate the membership program.

Nationwide Insurance has also used the Ratings and Reviews service of Bazzzarvoice.com to get the true picture of customers' requirements. The reviews not only show the customers' trust, they

114

also help them choose the correct policy that best meets their individual needs (http://reviews.nationwide.com/6951/1000/reviews.htm?pageNumber=115).

TIP: Other e-commerce sites, such as PowerReviews, Buzzillions, Wize and Reevoo, also provide ratings and review services, but Bazaarvoice is truly the leader in this space.

QUESTION AND ANSWER FORUMS

Have you ever noticed that if you don't answer the question of a potential customer, you often lose the sale? That's why a Question and Answer forum is fast becoming a useful business tool. It is a means of increasing communication between the company and the consumers.

There are two categories of customers who would not ask a question—one who knows nothing (and hence is not going to buy your product) and the other who knows everything (and hence can make a decision on his own). All others will likely have some questions. If these questions are answered well, you can easily get a sale and happy customers. There is a service by Bazaarvoice called Ask and Answer which helps your customers ask questions and you get the sales. They claim that you get two immediate benefits out of it:

Increase in sales—According to statistics from Bazaarvoice, (http://www.bazaarvoice.com/resources/case-studies/increase-sales/383-aa-conversion), with one question answered, sales conversion increases by 18.26%. If a consumer asks two questions, the conversion rate increases by 22%. You can compare your numbers with the investment that you will be making to get an application like this installed on your website and check what wonders it can do to your business.

115

Decrease in product return—When the customer is more confident about what they are buying, the chances of returning the product is greatly reduced.

The Home Depot of Canada is an online store for products related to home improvements, home renovation, tools, and hardware. It has Answer Depot (http://www.homedepot.ca/webapp/wcs/stores/servlet/DisplayTemplate?catalogId=10051&display=answer_depot&langId=-15&storeId=10051), in which customers can ask and answer questions. The unanswered problems are solved by the customer care team. For every category of product, there is a list of questions with answers that you get to see as you scroll down the page. This is a wonderful method of letting the customers know more about the products of the company.

Halford's (http://answers.halfords.com/answers/4028/allquestions.htm), the leading retailer of car maintenance and leisure products in the UK, used the question and answer application of Bazaarvoice and found that the conversion rate of customers who asked questions online is 58% higher than those who did not. The numbers seem to be quite promising irrespective of which industry you operate in.

STORIES

Interesting and authentic stories of consumer experience, when they are dealing with your business, can be a useful tool to engage others like them at an emotional level. They give you word-of-mouth publicity that customers tend to trust. They give you qualified leads and increase your search traffic. Bazaarvoice has been involved in calculating the ROI (Return on Investment) that the companies gain through its story sharing application. Names of other companies have been included in the relevant section.

116

La-Z-Boy, which is a leading home furniture company, ran a contest on its website to drive traffic. It was called 'Comfort Story' (http://stories.la-z-boy.com/stories/4276/product/test/stories.htm?scrolltotop=true).

Customers were asked to share a story about how La-Z-Boy added comfort to their lives. The prizes ranged from a $3,000 room makeover to a recliner valued at $600. Apart from that, there was a variety of small prizes as well. This campaign produced a remarkable increase in traffic to the website. More than 2,700 stories were entered and 38,500 visitors registered to the site, either to share a story or vote for a story. After the campaign ended, the company saw an 8% increase in its natural web traffic and an increase in sales.

Zale's, the jewelry retailer, asks its customers to share their real life stories, whether emotional and humorous, in which a purchase from Zales played a role. The contest is run through its love stories website (http://lovestories.zales.com/). The research shows that consumers who share their stories become emotionally bound with the company and are more likely to make repeat purchases. This is leading to increase in sales and loyalty of the customers.

TIP: Some other companies providing this capability are Reality Digital, which provides a storing and sharing platform, and Joomla, which provides recommendation and personalization.

BLOGS

Blogs are being extensively used to share information about the company, its products, and the industry. A blog is an excellent tool to increase consumer awareness and brand recognition.

On its blog Thousand Words (http://1000words.kodak.com/) Kodak informs consumers about new products and shares employee experiences stories from customers who let others like them know all they can do with a photograph. Customers are also asked to post their feedback on the images and their comments, ideas, and questions.

Dell's blog, Direct2Dell (http://en.community.dell.com/blogs/direct2dell/), is a good platform for product awareness, consumer training, learning, and discussing. There is a Shop section in which consumers can learn about products they can buy for home or office requirement, and a Participate section where visitors can discuss, view videos, read a blog, and share their views. The Support section is meant for customer service, and in another section visitors can learn about the company. Hence, there is great opportunity for interacting with the consumer.

There is no sure formula for calculating ROI from the blogs. It depends on the goal of the blog. ROI is directly related to the benefits that you are getting. The common benefits that companies agree to have achieved from these blogs are:

- increased sales,

- increased brand visibility,

- savings from customer's inputs, and

118

- reduced impact of negative content from the users.

You can calculate the cost of gaining these benefits by considering the costs involved in advertising on TV channels (to get customers views), publishing material in the press (to get the customer's stories published), hiring a buzz agent (to get word-of-mouth publicity), market research (against savings from customer's insight), and historical changes in sales due to change in a promoter type metric (to reduce the impact of negative user content). The total of these costs is the return you get by maintaining a blog.

A General Motors employee used the above calculation for calculating the ROI figure for its Fastlane blog (http://fastlane.gmblogs.com/). This blog is meant for discussions between GM leaders and the customers regarding cars and trucks. A GM employee found that there are 100 comments from its customers on the blog every month. The discussion led to customer insight regarding the product. To gain the same insight through the traditional method, the company would require a focus group that would cost it $15,000 a month or $180,000 a year. This is the ROI it is getting by maintaining the blog.

TIP: Before starting a blog, first decide what you want to achieve from the blog. Then it will be easier for you to calculate the ROI from the blog.

SETTING UP EXTERNAL SOCIAL MEDIA TOOLS ON YOUR WEBSITE

Before we talk about how to use these tools, let's discuss how to set them up on your website, one by one.

TWITTER

There are several applications available on Twitter that help to integrate this tool with your website, blog, or any HTML page.

The easiest way to get Twitter on your website is the Twitter Widget. Your latest tweets will appear on the sidebar of the website/blog for your visitors to read.

Another easy option is the Twitter Button, which appears on your website or your blog and promotes your Twitter account. You can choose from about forty versions of the button.

The application called Twitter Tools can create a blog post out of every tweet, a daily digest of the tweet posts, or a tweet for each of the blog posts.

Tweet Meme keeps track of the most popular links on Twitter at five-minute intervals. The more often a link has been tweeted, the higher its rank.

Twit is a promotional application that helps in creating Twitter fans and followers from those who like your blog posts. It appears as a small button placed on the blog, which readers can use to share what they are reading with other followers. Tweet, a WordPress plugin, is similar to Twit This.

Another WordPress plugin is TweetSuite, which shows the total conversation around a blog post. The third WordPress plugin is Chirrup, which allows you to show all the references from Twitter on the website.

Twitterfeed automatically insert tweets into your Twitter stream from any RSS feed. Hence your Twitter followers can be informed about the latest posting on the blog. You can also customize the format of the tweets generated.

Intense Debate is meant for threaded commenting, while Aweber is for tweeting a newsletter.

Very soon we will have Twitter @anywhere, a set of frameworks that lets you start an open discussion from any website. The website owners need to drop a few lines of javascript for the visitors to start a discussion.

LINKEDIN

In the year 2007, LinkedIn developed an API and widgets that can feed LinkedIn to your website and vice versa through the LinkedIn website (http://developer.linkedin.com). Through this website, LinkedIn has given a plethora of possibilities for integrating LinkedIn with your website or other social media tools. For example, Tweetdeck is well integrated with LinkedIn. Now one can see the updates of profiles of LinkedIn through Tweetdeck.

FACEBOOK

Here are some interesting Facebook statistics:

- Eight hundred forty-five million monthly active users at the end of December 2011.

- Approximately 80% of monthly active users are outside the US and Canada.

- Four hundred eighty-three million daily active users on average in December 2011.

- More than 425 million monthly active users who used Facebook mobile products in December 2011.

- Facebook is available in more than 70 languages.

(Source: http://newsroom.fb.com/content/default.aspx?NewsAreaId=22)

With Facebook Connect, any website can integrate Facebook API's for user authentication, website content sharing, publishing stories, and generating traffic.

Sociable Labs analyzed more than 1.35 million clicks via 42 different social sharing apps between October 2010 and January 2012 in order to determine the benefits and value of Facebook Connect users to retailers' websites.

The company defined Facebook-connected users in two ways:

- Those who used social log-in alternatives, such as "log in with Facebook" buttons, and

- Those who clicked on e-commerce sites' calls to action, which required them to share information from their Facebook accounts.

The software vendor concluded:

Based on its results, Facebook-connected users provide significant ongoing value to retailers, as these users continue to engage and share at very high rates on return visits.

Given this fact, the natural conclusion is that retailers should find engaging social experiences that motivate shoppers to connect, driving significantly higher LTV (lifetime value) through ongoing new customer referrals.

Beyond adding *Like* buttons and other social sharing features, you should consider adding a social log-in alternative to your site. Plus, consider adding the number of Facebook-connected users as a key performance indicator for your social strategy.

(Source: http://www.allfacebook.com/facebook-ecommerce-sites-2012-02)

> *TIP:* Refer to this article on Social Media Examiner that has helpful tips on Social Media integration: http://bit.ly/smeintegration.

A Facebook Connect widget, Fan Box, can bring content from the Facebook page to the website, and the website visitor can become a Facebook fan. Coca Cola uses Fan Box to convert visitors of its site into Facebook Fans. Other companies doing the same are Newsweek, ABC News, BlackBerry, NPR, and Herbal Essences.

There are a number of business card apps, such as Tag Biz Pro Business Card. Introductions Application helps you ask for introductions to lawyers, programmers, web designers and other professionals. My Office is for managing projects, scheduling meetings and group discussions, and assigning tasks.

YOUTUBE

YouTube gets 100 million views per day, or 3 billion views every month. It has led to some popular video campaigns. Skating Babies is one such campaign, which is the most viewed online advertisement. .

YouTube has effective API's and widgets that can help you integrate its videos and functionalities on the website.

Once integrated with a website, Data API can help you search and upload videos, create a playlist, and show related videos. Player API, which includes Embedded Player API and Chromeless Player API, allows you to control the look of the YouTube video on your website. Embedded Player is the easiest to use while Chromeless Player requires experience in web programming. Gaia online (http://www.gaiaonline.com/) the website for teenagers' fun, friendship, and games uses Chromeless API and Data API.

A Custom Player allows you to customize the YouTube Player and choose the video that you want to be played on your website. You can also create a list of favorite videos. You can have control over your website even when you are not able to edit it.

Widgets are meant for those who know HTML and JavaScript. The two widgets available are Video Bars and Video Search Control.

YouTube Direct is a more advanced API with which you and the visitors of your websites can directly submit videos on YouTube. This feature is used in Casio Exlim cameras where the video shoot can be loaded directly to YouTube through the website.

The most advanced API is the Developer Dashboard. It shows you the number of API and playback requests, uploads, and the various errors that your application generated. You need to have a developer key for that.

The ISP company Helio has a custom YouTube application through which the viewers can rate, comment, share, save, subscribe, record, and upload their videos.

Tip: Here is a link to see some of the most watched videos on YouTube>: http://www.readwriteweb.com/archives/top_10_youtube_videos_of_all_time.php

---

USING SOCIAL MEDIA TOOLS FOR YOUR BUSINESS

Let's now discuss how you can use these social media tools for gaining business.

TWITTER

Twitter is meant for real-time action. It's like coming to a cocktail party—lots of fun and action. The tone of conversation is casual to semi-formal. Not everyone is blessed with the skill to write long blogs. As Twitter microblogs have a 140-character limit, it's easy for anyone to communicate what they have in mind. Everyone can become a participant and mingling becomes easy. As the CEO of Zappos said, "Twitter is a great way to connect to the employees and customers at a more personal level."

According to a report published on Gartner Newsroom (http://www.gartner.com/it/page.jsp?id=920813), there are four ways by which companies are using Twitter for their benefit. They are:

Direct—Twitter can be used for direct marketing or as a public relations channel. It works like an extension to their corporate blog. It is used to announce corporate achievements, press releases, and other promotions. This is an easy way to get started. However, the tone of this kind of conversation is usually formal, whereas the people at Twitter like a personal touch. They do not like to hear self-praising words, so if you regularly use this approach, it can damage the reputation of your company. You can take lessons from   , which has been successfully promoting new products through Twitter (http://twitter.com/mystarbucksidea).

Indirect—Your employees tweeting about your company provides indirect communication through Twitter. The employees enhance their own and the company's reputation. They can tweet about their work, developments in the industry, the latest products in the market, and other things that your clients may be interested in. However, employees' tweets also have the power to tarnish the image of your company. This happened with Yahoo, when its employees tweeted throughout a layoff period. JetBlue (http://twitter.com/jetblue), Zappos, and Dell are using Twitter profiles for customer service. Southwest Airlines (http://twitter.com/southwestair) uses it for entertaining discussions.

Internal—Some companies use Twitter for their internal purposes. Employees can share their ideas and have threaded discussions on projects they are working on. However, this kind of talk should not be held in public. The better option for this kind of discussion is Yammer (https://www.yammer.com) which is meant for secure official microblogging.

Inbound signaling—Some companies use Twitter for listening rather than speaking. They might be using the tool search.twitter.com or the desktop application TweetDeck. They listen to what is being said about the company, what is happening in the industry, or how its product has been taken by the consumers. They tune in to these tweets to get early signals of anything alarming or any new wave that hits the market. Whole Foods Market (http://twitter.com/wholefoods) questions its customers on their reading, TV, and food habits.

It's not just the big businesses that can benefit by using Twitter. Small businesses can search tweets related to their brands and get to know that customers are happy using their products. There they can get a chance to share some tips regarding their product and enhance customer satisfaction. If there is some minor complaint that did not reach you, you can address them and surprise your followers. For bigger complaints, you can offer customer service and stop the negative words from being spread.

FACEBOOK

When we are talking about Facebook, we are talking about the personal space of real people who share their real feelings with their family and friends. Here is how you can use it for your business:

Marketing—There are several companies who use the Facebook marketing solution for advertising and brand promotion. Small companies do the same through Fan Pages. Starbucks, BMW, Toyota, and Coca Cola are a few of a long list of companies using Facebook for marketing. However, you must remember that Facebook is a kind of permission marketing.

Sharing Information with Customers – The Facebook wall is being used for updating customers with the latest product information and what's happening in the industry.

Recruitment—Companies have been hunting graduates by going through their Facebook profile to fill potential vacancies. Many fresh college graduates will not have a profile on LinkedIn yet, so it is useful to search through Facebook profiles as well.

Customer Service—Facebook pages can also be used to resolve customer service issues; however, you need to be aware that an irate customer will use any medium possible to be heard. Having an established policy and guidelines for Facebook Customer Service issues is essential.

Internal Communication—Though it is not advisable because of Facebook's open forum, a few companies use Facebook to communicate with their employees.

YOUTUBE AND OTHER VIDEO SITES

Web videos are a revolutionary way to make an effective social media presence. They let you inform, educate, and entertain your customers. To do this, all you need is a video camera and a good plan. Once the video is ready, you can post it to any of the popular video sites like YouTube, Utterli, Viddler, and Seesmic. Here's how you can use videos for your business:

Advertising—Advertising through videos has been a cost-effective method that you would definitely like to use in your company. BestBuy has been doing this successfully. Video advertising is especially useful for nonprofit organizations. However, you must remember to be creative enough in your videos, or else they will turn the viewers off.

How-to Videos—Home Depot has used how-to videos (http://www.youtube.com/user/homedepot?blend=2&ob=4&rclk=cti) to increase consumer awareness and education about using its products. The videos have created a reputation that Home Depot is there to help whenever you need assistance.

Product Demos—Instead of giving demos at the home of each and every customer or repeating the same demo several times in the retail outlet, place a product demo video on the Internet to be viewed by many users over and over again. This is extremely useful for companies selling software, mobile devices, and other gadgets with the latest technology. Companies like SalesForce, which sells software, has been successfully doing this. (http://www.youtube.com/user/salesforce). Online customers of Zappos have been finding the online shoe retailer's videos (http://www.youtube.com/user/zappos) useful. Sales conversion has increased by 6%-30%.

Consumer awareness—Virgin Airlines has been using its animated videos to tell about security measures that consumers need to take during the flight and in the event of a plane crash.

Connecting to your target—Videos are also used to connect to your target audience. This can be done even with simple entertainment. Check out Roxy's YouTube video (http://www.youtube.com/user/roxy?blend=1&ob=4&rclk=cti) for a great example.

Webinars—With a web camera installed in almost all the new PC notebooks, companies are finding it cost effective to hold web conferencing.

TIP: When you are creating a video, remember that it should

* have engaging, helpful content,

* have a clear focus,

* be high quality video,

* be short, and

* contain no hard selling.

LINKEDIN

LinkedIn is meant for the professional world. HR professionals from Hewlett Packard fill positions from sales to executive level through LinkedIn. According to a statistics published in the LinkedIn blog (http://bit.ly/linkedincorp), 40% of Fortune 100 companies use this tool for recruitment purposes. Some of the names on the list are Kraft, Intuit, ConAgra, EMC, and Allstate.

Companies have been using this tool for direct recruitment as well as for getting warm leads, referrals, background checks, and endorsements. Thus, they are saving on the cost of recruitment through consultants and job sites.

Some people successfully use this networking tool for sales. The professional connections built through this site are used by top marketing managers for making sales pitches to C-level management, not easily accessible otherwise. The software firm Software Traction Pty, Ltd is doing the same. If you have a business meeting scheduled with a person you have not met earlier, you can go through his or her LinkedIn profile ahead of time.

LinkedIn can also be a good platform for getting recommendation from clients and co-workers.

Some companies are also using LinkedIn for conducting surveys. If you do a traditional survey, the cost will be very high and hence asking questions in LinkedIn Answers can help you get good customer insight from professionals of any industry.

FLICKR AND PHOTOSHARING SITES

Photosharing sites like Flickr, Snapfish, or Photobucket have been used successfully as important pieces of the marketing strategy jigsaw. They have been used for advertising for the company, products, and services. Companies like Ford have been doing this successfully through Flickr (http://www.flickr.com/photos/fordmotorcompany/). The reason is that photos are supposed to be very human. When you are using a photo-sharing site for marketing or showing a brand presence, remember the following points:

- The name on the Flickr screen and your website should be the same. The graphics used should also be the same to give the feel of the integration of the two.

- The photos uploaded should be of high quality and related to your business.

- There should be text explaining the context of each photo; however, hard selling should be avoided.

- Find appropriate groups for joining and sharing your photos for brand promotion.

- There should be a prominent link on your website that would lead to your photostream.

- Be an active member of the Flickr community. Compliment photos posted by others, create a list of favorite photos, and take part in group discussions.

Fireman's Fund Insurance Company, a leading property and casualty insurance company, launched a photo-sharing campaign in which people were asked to share photos of architecturally and culturally significant places. The purpose was to make people aware of the national cultural heritage and motivate them for the preservation of these important buildings. The company was also getting brand awareness in this process of photosharing.

WEBINARS

Webinar is the name given to web-based seminars or web conferencing. This can be used to conduct live meetings, presentations, and training through the Internet. Webinar participants meet on the Internet through their web cameras instead of meeting in a conference room, and they speak over their mobile phones.

Webinars are becoming successful marketing tools for promoting a brand or products and marketing for a business. However, you can get the maximum out of it only when you cross promote it with your Twitter #hashtags, Facebook posts, LinkedIn profiles, and blogs. This way the news is spread to a larger audience and your message goes viral. Also, do not forget to upload the photographs of the Webinar on Flickr or some related live streaming videos.

Your customers and prospects may not always be able to attend a webinar because of scheduling conflicts. In that case, you want to record the webinar so it can be replayed at the convenience of the customers or prospects. Live Webinar Replay (http://www.buycbproducts.com/live-webinar-replay.html) helps you in recording and replaying webinars.

The top known vendors providing webinar services are
- VIA3 from Viack (http://www.via3.com/)
- Citrix GoToMeeting (http://www.gotomeeting.com)
- GoToWebinar (http://www.gotowebinar.com)
- WebEx (http://www.webex.com/)
- LiveMeeting (http://office.microsoft.com/en-us/livemeeting/default.aspx), and Acrobat Connect Pro (http://www.adobe.com/products/acrobatconnectpro/)

PODCASTING

Any broadcasting program (video or audio) made available online through RSS feed (or any other subscription feed) is called podcasting. Anyone who has the podcasting software and a simple microphone can record a show even at home.

Email advertisements often get caught in spam filters, and podcasting advertisements of your products eliminates that risk. You can edit the user list in the RSS feed to be able to set your target audience.

Consumers these days prefer buying from a company based on its values and mission. Instant communication plays an important role in letting people know about your company's values and in brand positioning among the young consumers who are techno-freaks.

Some of the leading podcast sites are iTunes, Podcast Alley, Zune, Odeo, and Podcast.com. For creating a podcast, you must know the process of recording an audio and saving it in MP3 file, the process of creating an RSS file which has the directions for sending the audio file to the user programs, writing directions in the RSS file, validating, and sending the file.

Following are the steps that you take for creating a podcast:

- *Prepare* a schedule for your program to be podcasted, be it daily or weekly.

- *Record* your show using software like Audacity (http://audacity.sourceforge.net/), then label and save the audio file as MP3 file.

- *Edit* the audio file for background noise and long periods of silence.

133

- *Prepare* an appealing intro for the program.

- *Create* the RSS podcast feed through your blog or some free service like FeedForAll: http://www.feedforall.com/.

- *Place* the RSS podcast on the Internet and *upload* your MP3 files.

- *Post* the file on your blog, making the title of the episode the title of the blog.

- *Submit* the episode to any podcast directory, such as iTunes.

- *Add* appropriate subscription buttons to your blog or website for an RSS feed.

- *Get* your podcast listed in various audio sites, such as Yahoo Audio Search.

There are some points that you must remember when creating your podcast. They are:

- When saying something that is to be podcast, do not stick to the script. It should be more from-the-heart communication.

- Be focused in what you are saying, which should be related to the products and services of your company or the industry.

- The first impression needs to be a good impression.

- On the basis of your customers' preferences, limit the length of your podcast.

- Learn to take the feedback on the face. Your response to negative feedback should also show your positive attitude.

Podcasting helps in grabbing attention to your business and building relationships with your listeners. If you are not confident that you can do a good job, hire an expert who has worked in this domain in the past.

It is amazing to see the spreading wave of social media. In one second, seven computers are sold in the world, 2.2 million emails are written and sent, two new blogs get created, 520 web links are clicked, 1,157 viewers watch a video on YouTube, and 31,000 messages are sent. This is nothing less than an explosion. If you still do not want to change with time, time will change you. Don't wait to hear success stories of your competitors—create your own!!

CHAPTER 8: SOCIAL MEDIA RISK MITIGATION

Risk management is an integral part of business, because the other face of the coin called *opportunity* is *risk*. So, when you are venturing into exploring the opportunities presented by social media, the chances of the other side of the coin showing up are just as great.

Instead of letting risks snowball into crises, the smarter move may be to anticipate most possible risks associated with social media and prepare ahead of time to deal with them or perhaps mitigate them completely. But in this context, you should also know that traditional risk management strategies cannot always alleviate many of the unique problems associated with social media. By the time you're finished with this chapter, you should have a fair idea about social media risk mitigation strategies that often require a *horses for courses* approach.

Social media risks can't be avoided but only mitigated.

As the saying goes, if you aren't in it, you can't win it! But the question is: at what cost will this victory from social media participation come? Well, the main threats that may arise from social media participation are:

- Not doing enough via social media or participating halfheartedly.
- Exposing your brand, assets, confidential data, and hard-earned reputation to possible harm. This encompasses legal risks as well.
- Getting engrossed in social media and neglecting your offline strategies.
- Becoming subject to regulatory or compliance risks (FTC, FINRA, etc.).

All of these risks are real, but, then again, no risk, no gain. So without further delay, let's take a closer look at some of the main risks that come with the territory.

> *TIP*: The main thing to remember is that social networking sites are not owned by you, and the websites can make changes to their policies. Bottomline, social media is social publishing. Don't post anything that you don't want your mom or your boss to see.

TO BE OR NOT TO BE...IS THAT THE QUESTION?

Have you ever tried to engage in a conversation while your attention is somewhere else? Well, if you have, you probably already know that such conversations are fruitless because you either end up saying the wrong things or saying nothing at all. When this happens, the person at the other end is less likely to re-engage in a conversation with you any time soon! Social media is no different.

Via social media, you start conversations with your customers, both present and potential, or perhaps join in conversations already in progress. But getting them to talk is no less important than keeping them talking. Only then will more people join in, and then you will create something viral. But, getting this free word of mouth requires considerable effort on your part, too.

Here are some potential dangers of not giving social media your best shot:

1. *When your message backfires.* Trying to start a conversation on a social media platform is about providing talking points to people. These talking points are what determine which way the conversation will head. So, before you write a blog, post a message on Twitter, or start a new thread on a forum, beware of the chain of events that your words can trigger.

Many a wily Internet marketer has failed with social media because they opted for the wrong message. Then again, there is always the risk of becoming the topic of the conversation while trying to become a part of it!

140

2. Not responding to feedback or responding inappropriately. The very act of engaging in social media is centered on the goal of generating customer feedback to improve products, services, and processes. But there is also a very potent risk involved with feedback. What happens when you don't respond to feedback in a timely fashion…or at all? Keep these things in mind when reviewing feedback:

Distinguish between a comment and a rant – Comments are worth listening and responding to and can help in alleviating negative buzz about your company. Rants, on the other side, are just rants, so grab a bag of chips and enjoy the playoffs.

Provide quick response on the same platform – The reason I use the word "quick" is because the timeliness is as important as the accuracy of the response. People expect near real-time response in social media. It's critical to respond quickly or else the effort loses its validity and impact.

Look at the feedback as an improvement opportunity –Negative feedback is as essential as positive and provides opportunities for improvement for your company. You should acknowledge the comment and respond back with your action plan, e.g., "We are considering your suggestion for our next product release." Again, be honest and transparent.

Patience is a virtue – Be patient and see if your supporters/advocates will chime in to protect you. The beauty of social media is that not all responses have to come from you and your customers can be your advocates.

You're NOT the only one – Believe me, yours is not the only company that gets negative comments, so neither get defensive nor overreact to the negatives. Just follow the other tips so that you shine over your competitors.

Prepare for the negatives – Lastly, as someone wisely said, "For every minute spent in organizing, an hour is earned." Yes, you can't be prepared for all the negative comments, but, some of them can be expected like:

- when a company makes a policy change, or

- new government legislative affects your industry, or

- you make changes in pricing/product features, etc.

Your public communication team can help you prepare some answers quickly or ahead of time so that you are in a much better state than being caught off guard.

So, that's that on negative feedback, now let's move on to how you need to handle positive feedback.

Respond to positive comments with thumbs up and all other social media kudos so that they keep coming. If you are indifferent to praise, there is a great risk of all appreciation drying up soon. And these are loyal customers that you are antagonizing, which renders your social media efforts counterproductive.

A simple acknowledgment is often enough to rub people the right way. But don't send out a standard response to every positive feedback you receive. A specific response shows people that you actually reviewed the praise before replying. This will help maintain the good vibes and also encourage positive feedback in the future. How about some other replies, like sending them gifts, special coupons, invitation to parties, game tickets, etc. without asking for any favor or positive comments. In fact, keep a list of such people for a brand ambassador program.

3. *Using social media halfheartedly, thus failing to generate enough interest* in your company on social platforms. If you are of two minds about

participating in social media or are not yet serious about it, how do you expect people to take an active interest in you on social media sites? At the end of it all, you may find yourself winding up your futile social media ventures after a great waste of resources.

Of course, it helps if you have a really popular presence in the real world and people think that you are the best thing since sliced bread! That way, popularity is not a problem and you may have a sea of fans and followers on your various social profiles. But most of us are not so lucky and have to work hard in building a faithful base of people interested in our social media presence. Luckily there are some ways in which you can mitigate the risk of your social media efforts collapsing due to the lack of public interest.

The best way you can draw people to your social media efforts is by organizing contests, sweepstakes, etc. It can work wonders in driving engagement and creating amazing word of mouth for your brand. Not only do social contests help in getting people talking about you, you can also get a bounty of customer information which you can utilize for future marketing purposes.

If you want a real-life example of how humor can be serious when it comes to social media, look no further than Zappos.com. This is an online shoe company that has "Create fun and a little weirdness" as one of its core values! And their CEO, Tony Hsieh, shows the way with regular tweets that can bring down the house with laughter: https://twitter.com/ZAPPOS.

You can get people interested in you with good clean humor, for which people can start loving you even before they try your products. Remember to:

- Poke fun at yourself, because it's the safest way to make fun without upsetting anyone. You will also earn a lot of brownie points that way.

- Point out the idiosyncrasies in your line of business or product line. People will join in and a huge conversation will soon ensue!

- Encourage the jesters out there to show their talent on your social media channels. Photos, videos, and articles are all welcome!

ThinkGeek (http://www.thinkgeek.com) is also a great example for understanding how you can use humor to create a fan following in social media. They use the above-discussed points to perfection in handling social media channels.

4. *Not achieving real-time participation.* A risk that is inherent in social media presence is that of not being able to achieve real-time participation. What is real-time participation? It is almost the same as engaging in a real-life conversation, where all participants pitch in with their statements one after the other. Since this is as easy online, via social media, you can at the most make sure that the conversation you are participating in has a flow and continuity about it.

For this you need good listening and engagement tools, because social media is not a spectator sport that can be egged on from the sidelines. You have to enter the ring! And unless you listen and engage proactively, your dream of real-time participation in conversations will remain just a dream!

Now that we have discussed the risks associated with improper social media efforts on your part, and also learned how to mitigate them effectively, it is time for you to know the risks you court even when you give social media your best shot.

THE PROBLEMS OF PUBLIC COMMUNICATION

Social media is still a concept that is very much in a state of rapid evolution. There are no set rules of the game, so you don't know when to call a foul. The initial problem that arises is one that involves confidentiality. If half of your employees participate in social media and yet do not understand this risk, they may be giving out more information than they should.

This is why you need to have effective social media guidelines for employees. While the presence of guidelines will not provide foolproof protection against mishandling of confidential information, guidelines will mitigate the risk of employees taking a wider berth than you actually meant them to have.

Moreover, employee guidelines for social media usage makes them understand the fact that they are representing the company in all their social media releases and the content of all such releases must be moderated so that they do not show the company in a bad light.

> *TIP*: Social Media is a publishing platform. You are not just sharing but publishing information on the Internet for your brand. It needs to be scrutinized like any other public communication platform.

We have already covered employee participation risks and the importance of social media usage guidelines for employees. Here are some companies whose social media guidelines can be a handy resource when you are trying to make your own:

Kodak: Employee education and understanding are of paramount importance if social media efforts are to succeed. Therefore, Kodak has built the company's social media policy around educating its employees about the indispensability of social media in today's business environment (http://www.kodak.com/US/images/en/corp/aboutKodak/onlineToday/Social_Media_10_7aSP.pdf). It talks about some of the most popular social media channels and provides user statistics for each. This educates employees about the various methods of successfully engaging in each of these social networks. In the same way, your employees can also understand the best practices for engaging both personally and professionally on various social media platforms.

Yahoo: Social media is not just a marketing tool but also a legal liability. So Yahoo has developed a company blogging policy that gives employees a full description of the risks of engaging in social media without restraint (http://jeremy.zawodny.com/yahoo/yahoo-blog-guidelines.pdf). The policy also suggests best practices so that no legal problems arise for the individual or the company. A similar approach can help you inform your employees of the potential dangers in clear terms but also show them the safe and productive ways of embracing social media.

General Motors: Transparency is the essence of successful social media usage by companies. The guidelines used by GM (http://www.conference-board.org/htmlEmail/pdf_files/Social-Media.pdf) focus on this fact. All their employees have to identify themselves as GM workers, whether or not their comments relate to the company. Anonymous posting is not allowed. They must also issue disclaimers that their views do not necessarily reflect that of the company. This can help you and employees conform to the recent FTC guidelines regarding social media.

Once a social media policy is in place, you are somewhat protected from the hazards of unregulated social media usage. Your employees now have a set of rules to play the game by and know when you can call a foul.

This brings us to the next social media risk you need to tackle: legal dangers.

BIG BROTHER IS WATCHING

Did you think that social media would forever be the Wild Wild West? With the popularity and impact of social media on commerce growing exponentially, the long arm of the law was bound to interfere in order to ensure that unethical practices were not taking place. This happened when the Federal Trade Commission (FTC) released a set of guidelines in 2009 that meant that some practices were rendered illegal by written law.

TIP: Watch this video: http://1.usa.gov/ftcguideline.

Social media enables you to use free word of mouth for mobilizing opinion in favor of your products and services. The importance of user-generated content such as reviews, blogs, tweets, etc., is such that the FTC felt that there should be more transparency in the way businesses are using this content. There were, after all, some advertisers who were misleading people by masquerading as independent users of their products.

In order to mitigate the risk of legal or regulatory action, *you must not*:

- *Engage in flogging* or creating blogs that promote your products and services without informing the readers that they aren't independent blogs.

- *Indulge in astroturfing* or posing as a user of your products on social media sites and writing rave reviews that influence others.

- *Pay social media users to post information* that is partially or entirely incorrect and may cause harm to those who trust such information.

147

- Moreover, if you are employing a celebrity or anyone else to write good things about you on sites such as Facebook and Twitter, they must reveal the details of such an endorsement contract. Failure to do this will invite legal action.

If you are already into social media, you may need to overhaul your policies to eliminate anything that won't pass through the FTC endorsement guidelines (http://business.ftc.gov/sites/default/files/pdf/bus71-ftcs-revised-endorsement-guideswhat-people-are-asking.pdf). This is the only way to mitigate the risk.

In a nutshell, here is the crux of the FTC guidelines:

- Endorsements must be truthful and not misleading;

- If the advertiser doesn't have proof that the endorser's experience represents what consumers will achieve by using the product, the ad must clearly and conspicuously disclose the generally expected results in the depicted circumstances; and

- If there's a connection between the endorser and the marketer of the product that would affect how people evaluate the endorsement, it should be disclosed. For example, if a product was provided for review at no cost, that should be disclosed.

> *TIP:* Read the following for more information:
>
> http://business.ftc.gov/documents/bus71-ftcs-revised-endorsement-guideswhat-people-are-asking
>
> http://business.ftc.gov/multimedia/videos/endorsement-guides
>
> If you are in the financial services industry, the guidelines (http://www.finra.org/web/groups/industry/@ip/@reg/@notice/documents/notices/p120779.pdf) issued by the Financial Industry Regulatory Authority, or FINRA, apply to you. This is a set of guidelines which governs the use of social media by firms and brokers.

Here are a few highlights:

- FINRA proposed that firms not need prior approval of content posted on social sites as long as the site qualifies as an interactive electronic forum.

- FINRA proposes to reduce the six categories of communications to three, as follows

  o Institutional communication: includes all communications that fall within the current guidelines.
  o Retail communication: includes any written (including electronic) communication that is made available to more than 25 retail investors within any 30-day period. "… Communication that currently qualifies as advertisements and sales literature would generally fall under the definition for retail communications."

○ Correspondence: includes any written (including electronic) communication that is distributed or made available to 25 or fewer retail investors within any 30-day period.

This is good news for firms and reps engaging in social media, since organizations will not need to review content posted to social networking sites in advance.

The following rules still apply:

- Companies must still maintain records of the communications as they are doing currently.

- Companies must supervise the content in the same manner as correspondence, which means firms must review the content after it's posted, so monitoring and mining capabilities on social networks is still important.

- Companies still can't predict performance, imply past performance will recur, or make any exaggerated or unwarranted claims, opinions, or forecasts. As the New York Times reported, a California broker was suspended and fined $10,000 in July for posting "misrepresentative and unbalanced" messages on Twitter.

TIP: Your social media profiles still need to be reviewed before publishing. You can read the entire submission here:

http://www.finra.org/web/groups/industry/@ip/@reg/@rulfil/documents/rulefilings/p123893.pdf.

TWO SIDES OF THE SAME COIN

Finally we come to the problems that may arise if you are too engrossed in your social media efforts and neglect your offline marketing activities. The risk here is that you will be losing out on major earning opportunities, because as you may know already, the real action takes place offline.

And more importantly, 90% of all conversations between people take place offline. So, simply being a part of the online conversations via social platforms will not help you make it big. So, you need to integrate your online and offline marketing efforts to get the best results.

Here are a few ways in which you can start promoting your social media presence offline:

- Have your Twitter #hashtag and links to your Facebook page printed on your business cards.

- In your ad campaigns, use a couple of lines telling people where to find you on social networks. You can, of course, provide incentives for people to look you up, but that may also attract the gold-diggers.

- For printed ads such as banners and billboards, you can use testimonials you have received online and also inform people about the latest goings-on in your social sites. Inform them of contests, sweepstakes, discounts, and whatever it is that you think will get them interested.

- You can even include links to your social profiles on your shopping bags and bills. So, every customer walking out of your store has the chance to become your fan or follower on the Web.

> *TIP*: The # symbol, called a hashtag, is used to mark keywords or topics in a Tweet. It was created organically by Twitter users as a way to categorize messages. More information: http://bit.ly/twitterhashtag.

In the same way, your social media releases can also boost the success of offline marketing campaigns. Your tweets can talk of a new store being opened, the latest discount schemes, loyalty bonuses for customers, and a lot more customer delights that they can only experience if they walk into your store and complete an actual transaction with you.

Companies have successfully mitigated the risk of not being able to integrate social media marketing with offline marketing campaigns. Here are some great examples that may show you the way ahead:

- In late 2009, Trident, the confectionery biggie, ran a full-page ad that consisted of several tweets (absolutely unedited) from fans of their new line of chewing gums. (http://www.convinceandconvert.com/wp-content/uploads/2009/12/trident-ad.jpg). The same ad also asked the readers to visit their Twitter profile. This way, they talked about themselves (as is done in all ads) but in a novel way that definitely generated more interest than an ordinary paper ad about a chewing gum ever would have!

- Naked Pizza, who's USP (Unique Selling Point), is healthy pizzas, put up billboards (http://tctechcrunch.files.wordpress.com/2009/04/twittersign.png) that urged people to follow them on Twitter for the best deals. In fact, they put up this sign right on top of their store in place of the regular "call for delivery" billboard. And you can be sure they turned heads!

So, you can clearly see that deploying user-generated content for advertising purposes is going to be really big soon, if not already. The logic is that if people can trust each other's opinions, reviews, recommendations, and warnings shared via social media, won't they do the same when such content is presented via conventional channels? They sure will and so you must not miss out on the opportunity.

Social media risk mitigation is a challenge you simply cannot avoid. By employing the right resources, creating and implementing ground rules and policies, training your employees, and giving them continuous support you can easily come out on top. Half the battle is won by knowing about those risks and the other half is won by effectively implementing risk mitigation strategies in your organization.

CHAPTER 9: MEASURE SOCIAL MEDIA—IS IT EVEN POSSIBLE?

So you have been through the difficult phase of change and finally, now, social media is an integral part of your organization. Just when you are ready to breathe a sigh of relief, you realize you need to 'measure' the results of your social media efforts. But considering that social media is still evolving, you may wonder whether it is actually possible to do that.

WHY IS MEASURING CRITICAL?

"You can't control what you can't measure." ~ Tom DeMarco

"Not everything that can be counted counts, and not everything that counts can be counted." ~ Albert Einstein

The reasons for measuring social media are no different from why you measure the success or failure of your other efforts at the end of every fiscal year. So, measurement is a must to:

- *Control the inputs*—Unless you assess the current status of social media in your organization, you will never be able to take control of the situation and make the necessary changes. Only by reviews, will you get to know the deviance that exists between your goals and actual achievement. Also, you get to understand why such deviation (if any) occurred and take steps to ensure that it does not happen again. Changes may be required in personnel, resources, or processes in order to make social media work better for you.

- *Impact the bottom line*—The most important financial objective behind measuring social media is to know whether it affects your bottom line. Sure, increasing your after-tax profits was not your primary objective of engaging in social media. But what if social media has helped increase the inflow of revenue substantially enough to affect the bottom line? This calls for measurement and thorough analysis, so that future social media engagement proves more fruitful. The reverse may also be true. What if organizational productivity has gone down due to the use of social media by your employees or the fact that you have ignored conventional marketing tools for this new age medium? In both cases, your bottom line may take a hit!

- *Adjust your social marketing mix*—When you started out with social media, you may have had only one or more strategies in place, with tactics to implement each of them. Measuring social media allows you to see which of those tactics has been the most effective. Are your Facebook or Twitter efforts gaining you more popularity, or are the full blogs doing more? Was your focus on social media contests fruitful or should you have used more offline tools to promote your social presence? For this kind of tactical analysis, measurement is a must.

- *Feed it back to your strategy*—And when you are doing tactical analysis, you cannot ignore the strategy as a whole either. Measurement will tell you what changes are to be made to the overall strategy, not just the tactic. So, the measurements allow you to detect profitable and achievable changes to your social media strategy. That's great, right?

- *Share your success story*—One more important reason for measuring social media is the fact that your stakeholders need information. You have spent a lot of time in selling the idea of social media to your stakeholders (employees, channel partners, franchisees, etc.), so it is also important to show them the report card. If you can present quantifiable proof that social media has indeed made a difference, then this will help you gain greater support from these stakeholders for future changes and decisions. Maybe you will not have to try so hard for building buy-in within your organization the next time!

- *Acquire funding for a social program*—The more you are able to show the value that social media is bringing, the better budget allocation can be done in the future. Also, it keeps the accountability high with every team in the social program.

- *Reflect your thoroughness and willingness to succeed*—Quite a few marketing efforts don't have well-defined metrics, or they've never been measured. Having a plan to measure your social media efforts demonstrates that you are thorough and focused on success.

- *Demonstrate that goals and objectives have been accomplished*—The metrics finally reflect how well you were able to achieve the goals and objectives for the social program. The metrics have to be aligned to the goals for the social program, and everyone will be able to see which goals have been met, which need improvements, and which need to be replaced.

TIP: The first step towards creating the social metrics is to have clear and tangible goals and objectives. The ROI in social media is both Return on Investment and Return on Influence.

SOCIAL MEDIA: WHAT TO MEASURE?

Broadly, what you are measuring is return on investment. This investment has been in terms of more products/services, more customers, and greater customer retention. There are also intangible efforts. You need to find out whether they have given you enough returns from social media participation. But evaluating return on investment is also important to find out whether the opportunity cost is too high.

Returns from investment in social media are basically outcomes of your effort. It is very important that you differentiate between outcomes and output when measuring social media.

So what is the difference? As you can see, *outputs* are usually tangible and can be seen and felt. If you can get your hands on it, it's probably an output from some process.

An *outcome* is a level of performance or achievement. Outcomes quantify performance.

So, when you cook a meal for your family, the output is a well-cooked meal. But it can have multiple outcomes:

- You feel happy because you like to cook for your family.

- Your family enjoyed the meal.

- The food was ready by dinner time.

See, with social media, it is very important to measure outcomes and not just outputs. One of the outputs of introducing social media in your organization may be that 500 employees get actively involved, but the outcome is that it increases employee satisfaction and overall brand sentiment for your company. OR the resolution of ten customer service complaints a week is the output, and the outcome was eight customers retained and improved brand sentiment in the market.

For social media platforms, the number of followers, number of fans, number of re-tweets, number of posts, number of likes, and similar numbers are outputs and the outcomes from that will be knowing your customers, better understanding of their needs, and, finally, improving products, services, processes, and online experiences to cater to their demands.

Similarly, for social media, there may be multiple outcomes, and the only way to know whether you are progressing in the right direction is to measure those outcomes. But if you measure outputs, such as how many online contests you've had and how many blogs posts you've made, you may fail to see the bigger picture.

And measuring the outcomes of social media involvement periodically will also help you establish trends, which is perhaps the best way to track the long-term potential of social media. The key is to measure to determine whether your social media efforts have produced *significant outcomes and not just substantial outputs.*

Now that you understand the difference between outputs and outcomes, let us take a more specific look at what to measure in social media.

> *TIP:* Processes deliver outputs; performance drives outcomes.

Since we have talked about Return on Investment (*ROI*), you need to be absolutely clear that it is a business metric and not a media metric. So why measure ROI at all? This is simply because measuring social performance alone will not get you anywhere. At the end of the day, even immense social media success is of no use if you are not creating new business for your brand, especially since your company is now more popular or valuable than it was before.

You will allocate resources in the future only where you can make money. If social media isn't doing that, then you may want to seriously look at where you are going wrong. The non-financial outcomes of your social media efforts are not ROI. So, positive or negative word of mouth, Twitter followers, Facebook fans, likes, and Diggs are not where your measurement process ends. Of course you are measuring them and you should—measuring impressions and eyeballs is the best way to know whether you are headed south with your social media efforts. But measuring ROI is imperative.

It may surprise you, but a survey by emarketer.com found 84% of businesses that have adopted social media do not measure the ROI of their social endeavors. And more than 40% even said that they are not sure whether this can be done at all! If these companies do not indulge in some serious process correction, they may soon be limiting their social media efforts due to the failure to find tangible returns on investment.

This brings us to how social media can be measured.

SOCIAL MEDIA MEASUREMENT: HOW TO GO ABOUT IT

Okay, now we are at the most important part of it all: performing the actual measurement.

The best approach is to measure both quantitative and qualitative outcomes.

As far as qualitative outcomes are concerned, they may be of various types, such as brand value and perception, customer engagement, and better relationships with customers and the public. Even qualitative research can have success metrics like:

Loyalty: Amount of positive comments and conversations per week generated by social media.

Sentiment Analysis: See if you can increase positive mentions of your brand after you start participating in social media.

Innovation: New ideas generated and beta testing done before releasing to production.

Research and Feedback: Improvements made to products based on social media feedback. Number of market research questions answered on social media platforms.

Advocates: Finding and cultivating brand advocates who will promote your business for you. According to a study conducted by Eloqua in January 2011 (http://blog.eloqua.com/social-engagement-and-nps/), socially engaged customers are highly likely to be brand advocates:

- Customers who post about Eloqua in its LinkedIn User Group are more than three times more likely to be promoters than its baseline customer.

- Customers who comment in its Facebook Fan page are seven times more likely to be promoters than its baseline customer.

- Customers who tweet about Eloqua are a whopping nine times more likely to be promoters than its baseline customer.

- Overall the NPS (Net Promoter Score) for customers who engage with Eloqua on social channels is 450% higher than its average NPS.

Sharing: How many times social content has been shared. Tools like addthis.com (http://www.addthis.com),
sharethis.com (http://www.sharethis.com),
share.lockerz.com (http://share.lockerz.com/),
socialtwist.com (http://www.socialtwist.com), etc., have good analytics capability that can give reports on such metrics.

There can be several such questions that you can use to measure the impact of social media on your organization, each relating to the goals you started with. These qualitative measurements are done by professionals who engage in detailed human analysis to find out where you stand on various social platforms.

Plus these days, Twitter is big. You should know that there are some great tools for measuring the qualitative outcome of your Twitter presence. You will surely agree that unless you know whether the Twitter mentions about your brand or product are positive or negative, they are not that useful. This requires *sentiment analysis*, which is important because social sentiment can be used as a parameter for judging the level of engagement your social presence has created.

Some social sentiment measurement tools are
- Viral Heat (http://www.viralheat.com/)
- Twendz (http://twendz.waggeneredstrom.com/)
- Tweet Feel (http://www.tweetfeel.com/)
- Crimson Hexagon (http://www.crimsonhexagon.com/)

So if you are into microblogging, you must make good use of these tools.

On the other hand, there's the challenge of measuring quantitative outcomes, ones which can be termed as returns on investment, in the strict monetary sense of the term. Here are some Key Performance Indicators (KPIs):

- Website traffic

- Search engine rankings

- Increase in number of customers

- Increase in products/services

- Bounce rates

- Customer retention

> *TIP*: Social media efforts should increase your consideration rate, which in turn affects your conversion rate.

Consideration is the penultimate step before the buyer makes the final decision to buy and is evaluating all options. Consideration rate is the percentage of people who are "considering" their options before making the final purchase.

Conversion rate is the percentage of people who 'convert" from potential buyers to actual buyers.

And then there are specific aids to measure quantitative outcomes, such as sales, website traffic, or SEO (Search Engine Optimization) rankings:

- *Google Analytics* (http://www.google.com/analytics): This works for a variety of purposes, not just search engine rankings. There is no better way of tracking the activities of users who have reached your social profile via incoming links

- *Omniture* (http://www.omniture.com/en/products/analytics): Has several services available for businesses to utilize. If you are looking to measure Facebook and Twitter ROI, this is the tool you need.

- *TweetMeme Analytics* (http://tweetmeme.com/): This helps you take an in-depth look at your achievements on Twitter.

- *PostRank Analytics* (http://analytics.postrank.com/), acquired by Google: This suite of tools helps you measure social engagement on various social networking platforms. This resource allows you to enter a feed URL and obtain various useful stats about sharing of content on various social networking sites.

SOCIAL METRICS TOOLS AND SERVICES

The importance of measuring social media can be understood by looking at how businesses are benefiting from doing so. There is a whole host of companies that offer you smart solutions to your social media management problems. The biggest names in the corporate realm are using these solutions. If you want to have your social media efforts measured professionally, these resources are your best bet.

1. *Spredfast* (http://www.spredfast.com): This is one of the best social media management platforms around. It allows you to manage, monitor, and measure your presence on various social media channels. So, it helps you with the entire process and not just the measurement part of it.

By using Spredfast, you can distribute your branded content between various social channels and maintain control over them via a unified dashboard. As far as measurement of your media efforts is concerned, Spredfast can give you a detailed ROI analysis. You can benefit from features such as:

- *The analysis of channel effectiveness*: This helps you understand which social channels are working for you and which are not. So, in the future, you can focus more on the channels that are better fits for your social media initiatives.

- *Activity trend:* What kind of engagement and participation has your social presence been able to generate? Certain key performance indicators help you measure this for every social channel.

- *Downloadable data*: Spredfast allows you to have all the data relating to your social media measurement on your computer on a spreadsheet. So when you are preparing a report on your social media ROI, you can use this data the way you want to!

2. *EmPower Research* (http://www.empowerresearch.com): This company provides customized social media intelligence to businesses all over the world. Its USP (Unique Selling Point) is multi-country and multi-lingual social media analysis. Its global presence and success is reflected by the fact that it counts Fortune 100 companies such as Nokia among their clients.

So, what can EmPower Research offer you? Well, quite simply, a bouquet of services and solutions as integral social media support. But if you want specific measurement services, you have:

a.) *Media measurement:*

- *Metrics* which tell you how your intended message was received or perceived by the target audience. This will help you streamline your messages for better congruency with your image or product.

- *Useful qualitative analytics* such as type of hits, share of volume and reach, tonality, etc.

b.) *Market intelligence via social media measurement*: By utilizing structured data such as social media literature surveys, you can get actionable insights into your media initiatives and make improvements wherever necessary. These insights can be about your products/brands and consumers as well as about where you stand in the industry with respect to the usage of social media.

EmPower Research offers measurement solutions in the form of the Global Listening Model. This comprises proprietary technology and methods that enable you to drive ROI and make key social media engagement decisions. Depending upon your level of social media engagement, this EmPower solution can help you:

- *Track* the volume of conversations across various social channels.

- *Measure and analyze* the qualitative aspects of the conversations.

- *Gauge* the impact of viral marketing efforts on social platforms.

As you may have guessed by now, the strength of this company lies in its methodologies. So, if you are looking for a professional social media measurement mechanism, you can get the very best because EmPower has:

168

- *Analytics+:* An engine wherein conventional quantitative data from market trends is combined with qualitative social media data to provide greater insight.

- *SMMART or Social Media Multi-Attribute Rating Tool*: This tool allows you to rank sites based on their popularity on social platforms.

- *Corporate and Brand Equity and Reputation Trackers*: This helps you understand how social media is helping elevate the status of your brand among customers, present and potential, as well as other stakeholders. The trackers are unique because they use a 360-degree measurement approach.

3. *Social Media Insights* (http://www.jdpower.com/business-services/services/social-insights.htm): The USP of this J.D. Power and Associates tool is to "bring the consumer to life with social media analysis." The company can measure social media in a way that provides not only data, but also insights into consumers, brands, and trends. The results provided by this tool are segmented by demographics and psychographics.

Some advanced things users can do with this tool:

- Product Launch Assessment
- Campaign Impact Assessment
- Category Driver Assessment
- Competitive Brand Assessment
- Shopper Experience Assessment
- Social Media Benchmarking
- Social Media Intelligence

169

Umbria also focuses on measuring the impact of blogs, because according to it, bloggers are opinion leaders and can indicate mass trends of the future.

4. *Radian6* (http://www.radian6.com): The company promises a complete platform for measuring and engaging in social media. It provides a flexible dashboard that helps you monitor all forms of social media with real time reports and measures. Radian6 provides you the unique opportunity of filtering and segmenting your social media data before measuring it through various lenses. What's more, Radian6 can even help you measure newer social channels such as Google Buzz.

If you choose Radian6, you get benefits such as:

- Evaluation of individual viewpoints and their impact on your brand within a social channel.

- Analysis of the most impactful conversations.

- Measurement of the lifecycle of buzz, so you can understand how much effort should go into specific promotions on social platforms.

Pepsi, Microsoft, Kodak, and AMDA are some of Radian6's clients. So, you'll be in elite company for sure!

5. *TwelveForce Media* (http://www.twelvefold.com/): This company, formerly Buzzlogic, understands that conversations on social space equal to brand impact. It helps you place your ads on sites where conversations are tailor-made for giving your brand the boost you are looking for. And then it helps you in measuring the results of such actions.

If you are looking to measure social media influence, trust TwelveForce Media with the job. By indexing 7,300 media sources, social sites, and corporate websites, the company helps you understand how many sites your content reaches with relevance intact.

6. *Cymfony* (http://www.cymfony.com): By combining a powerful social media listening platform with unparalleled market intelligence delivery, Cymfony tells you what you need to know about your social media efforts. The patented Verismo methodology used by Cymfony helps you understand the key drivers to brand growth on social networks by using simple but powerful metrics.

7. *Nielsen BuzzMetrics* (http://bit.ly/nielsenbuzzmetrics): A discussion about media measurement without bringing Nielsen into it would be a travesty. Buzzmetrics, the social media measurement wing of Nielsen, delivers brand metrics and insights to help you understand the impact of user-generated content on social platforms. It helps you measure content from a whopping 100 million blogs, forums, social networks, groups, boards, and other platforms! This is particularly useful in tracking and measuring specific social media campaigns and devising a strategy that will serve you well in the future.

> *TIP*: Look for tools that can incorporate metrics from a variety of platforms with flexibility to adapt to new platforms that fit your budget.

Social media measurement is constantly changing as existing platforms evolve and new ones enter the social space. One thing that remains the same is keeping an eye on data and creating meaningful Key Performance Indicators (KPIs).

CHAPTER 10: MOBILE SOCIAL MEDIA

So what's the next big thing in social media? What will be the next Facebook or Twitter, taking social media to a whole new level? While it's really difficult to make these predictions, there's something big that's already in the making. It's social media on mobile devices. You may not be aware, but the wheels are in motion and usage of mobile phones for accessing social networks, blogs, forums, communities, message boards, and microblogging is on the rise. As a matter of fact, according to a recent survey by eMarketer (http://www.emarketer.com/Article.aspx?R=1006255), more than 800 million people worldwide will be using their mobile phones for accessing social platforms by 2012. And this number was a measly 82 million just two years ago! So, if this is not the next big thing, what is?

In this chapter, I will try to dissect this phenomenon to find out the causes and effects of increased usage of mobile phones for social media. We will also try to look into the crystal ball and find out what lies ahead for this trend.

MOBILE DEVICES AND SOCIAL MEDIA: A MATCH MADE IN HEAVEN

What is social media about? It's about keeping in touch despite distances, creating conversations we love, and having the globe within easy reach. So, quite clearly the use of social media was never going to be restricted to the PC or the laptop, because they offer limited mobility at best. And if you cannot remain in touch with your friends, family, co-workers, clients, and business partners 24x7, what's the use of social media?

The concept of social media and the underlying principles behind the success of mobile phones mirror each other to some extent at least. This is because you need both to stay connected. Being without a mobile phone for an hour and not using social media for a day or two can evoke the same emotional response, a feeling that you are cut off from the rest of the world. Maybe the yearning for social media has not yet reached that level where you can call it a necessity, but that day is not far off either. For now, mobile phones have allowed you to access social media whenever you like, from wherever you want.

In fact, the purchase decisions of 38 million 13- to 80-year-olds in the US are now influenced in various ways by social media—up 14% in just six months.

The results come from Wave 2 of The Faces of Social Media[SM] Research, (http://www.knowledgenetworks.com/resources/faces.html), which provides a consumer-centric view of social media involvement and its effects on 39 product categories. The syndicated study, focused on the marketing consequences of social media ("SoMe"), is a joint research venture of Knowledge Networks (KN) and MediaPost Communications' Center for Media Research.

Teens and adults who were social media users in 2011 reported high levels of influence as follows:

- *23.1 million* discovered new brands or products through social media (up 22% from 2010).

- *22.5 million* used SoMe to learn about unfamiliar brands or products (up 9%).

- *17.8 million* were strongly influenced in their purchase decisions by opinions in social media (up 19%).

- *15.1 million* referred to social media before making purchase decisions (up 29%).

Consumers are also integrating social media usage with their mobile phone activity. In 2011, 40% of teens and adults who had ever used social media were accessing it through their mobile device—up from 28% from 6 months ago. *This means that roughly 80 million people check social media from a mobile device.*

As a result, social media is now a *wherever I am* option, integrated into the mobile-plus social media users' shopping experience and habits; 27% compare or check prices via social media, 24% refer to reviews for brands/places/services; and 16% (23% of Boomers) use social media to find coupons or other discounts for local businesses.
(Source: http://www.techjournalsouth.com/2011/06/social-media-affects-purchase-decisions-of-38m-americans-influence-growing/)

Usage of both mobile phones and social media is growing quickly, which perhaps helps create further synergy. An iPhone is sold every two seconds, ten new Twitter users surface every three seconds, and about ten new users access social media on mobile devices every second. The numbers are simply unbelievable, but they are true
(http://www.upsidelearning.com/blog/index.php/2009/10/26/the-social-media-and-mobile-computing-explosion/)!

And two of the most important benefits of this synergistic growth to the end users are:
1. A reduction in the price of smartphones, and
2. Newer and simpler social media apps for users of all ages and levels of gadget savviness.

The Google Android has also played its part in ushering a boom in the usage of social media on mobile. This is the operating system for smartphones other than the iPhone and the BlackBerry and powers a huge chunk of smartphone sales. Research firm comScore released December 2011 US mobile subscriber market share and found that Google's Android is leading with a 47.3-percent OS market share (rising 2.5 points) and Apple's iOS is in second with a 29.6-percent market share (rising 2.2 points).

Excerpt from the comScore report:

97.9 million people in the US owned smartphones during the three months ending in December, representing 40 percent of all mobile subscribers. Google Android ranked as the top smartphone platform with 47.3 percent market share, up 2.5 percentage points from September. Apple maintained its #2 position, growing 2.2 percentage points to 29.6 percent of the smartphone market. RIM ranked third with 16 percent share, followed by Microsoft (4.7 percent) and Symbian (1.4 percent).

Top Smartphone Platforms
3 Month Avg. Ending Dec. 2011 vs. 3 Month Avg. Ending Sep. 2011
Total US Smartphone Subscribers Ages 13+
Source: comScore MobiLens

Share (%) of Smartphone Subscribers

	Sep 11	Dec 11	Point Change
Total Smartphone Subscribers	100.0%	100.0%	N/A
	Sep 11	Dec 11	Point Change
Google	44.8%	47.3%	2.5
Apple	27.4%	29.6%	2.2

RIM	18.9%	16.0%	-2.9
Microsoft	5.6%	4.7%	-0.9
Symbian	1.8%	1.4%	-0.4

TIP: You can see the full comScore report here:

http://bit.ly/comscoremobile2011.

The team at Tatango compiled data from the Pew Research Centers Internet & American Life Project (http://bit.ly/pismartphone) and created the infographic on the next page.

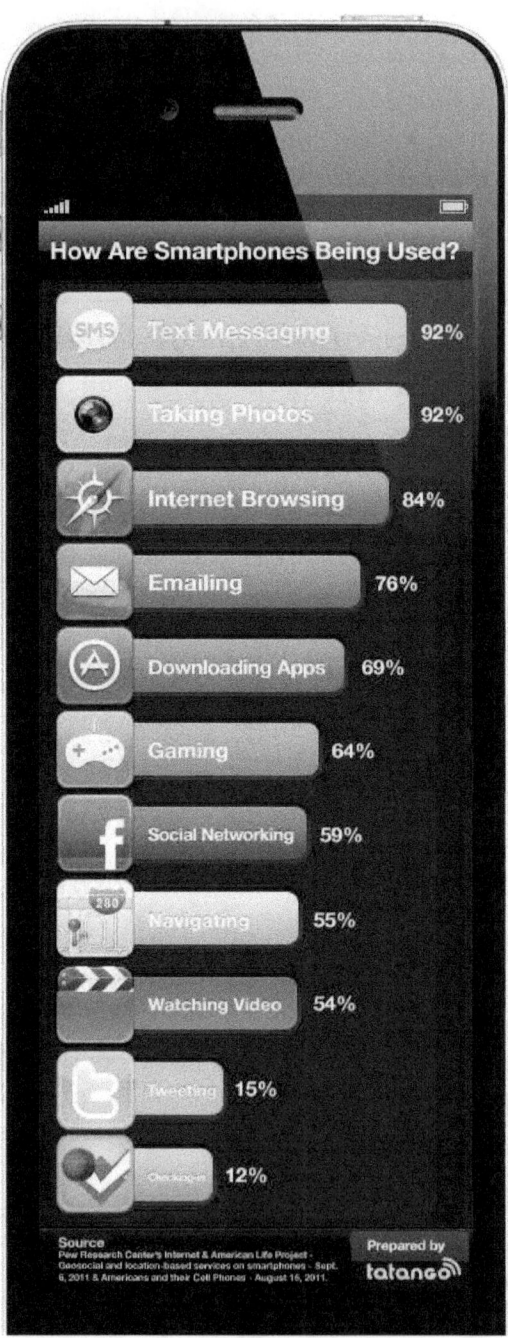

While the average session length still has some way to go before it catches up with the usage of other apps, you can be sure that the numbers for social media usage will keep on climbing, while the same may or may not be true for other apps.

This is because there is still a huge gap between the sales of smartphones in US and Europe and in some of the developing countries of Asia, particularly in the southeastern part of the continent. And there is huge potential for growth in these markets because a majority of the population is young, with a high propensity to spend, particularly on lifestyle goods such as smartphones. As per a recent Global Web Index survey (http://www.globalwebindex.net), countries like India and China will be pivotal in taking the boom of social media on mobiles to a whole new level, specifically due to this reason.

So, overall it looks like social media and mobiles have forged a very strong partnership!

WHAT'S ON OFFER?

A key question about the rise of social media on mobile platforms is: What does your smartphone have to offer when it comes to social media? Well, there are specific mobile phone features to support social media, but at the same time social media channels have also adapted themselves to fit perfectly into your pocket. In fact there are some social platforms specifically meant to be used on mobile phones.

There are also some other factors that need to be considered, without which the full power of the social media–mobile combo cannot be experienced:

- High speed internet via 3G /4G /4G LTE connections
- Affordable data usage plans

The markets where the use of social media on mobile devices has peaked are characterized by both of the above-mentioned attributes.

> *TIP:* What is LTE? An acronym for Long Term Evolution, LTE is a 4G wireless communications standard developed by the 3rd Generation Partnership Project (3GPP) that's designed to provide up to 10x the speeds of 3G networks for mobile devices such as smartphones, tablets, netbooks, notebooks and wireless hotspots. 4G technologies are designed to provide IP-based voice, data and multimedia streaming at speeds of at least 100 Mbit per second and up to as fast as 1 GBit per second.

However, when you look at the leaders in mobile social media, the names will not surprise you at all:

1. *Facebook Mobile*: This application allows you to upload photos and text from your phone to your Facebook page. You can receive and reply to Facebook messages, pokes, and wall-posts using the texting service on your phone or simply log onto http://m.facebook.com using a mobile browser. It works on all platforms, including Symbian and Windows mobiles.

And what do the figures say about the success of Facebook mobile? Well, Facebook is the most-accessed social site from mobile devices. According to Facebook, more than 100 million people access the site from mobile devices all over the world. That's almost a quarter of all Facebook users!

2. *Twitter*: This pioneering site for microblogging started its streamlined mobile interface, http://m.twitter.com, in 2007. Since the concept of Twitter is to use messages with 140 characters or less to update your status and stay connected, the use of this resource on mobiles seems just perfect.

And the numerous Twitter apps for mobile devices make Twitter the second most frequented social site on mobile phones, behind only Facebook. Some of the other most popular apps are the following:

TweetScope (www.tweetbot.com),

Twitterrific (http://twitterrific.com/),

and TweetDeck (http://www.tweetdeck.com/)

are some of the best iPhone Twitter apps.

œTwit (http://www.kosertech.com/cetwit-info/)

and rowi (http://hiddenpineapple.com/rowi),

are Windows mobile applications.

Plume (http://levelupstudio.com/plume), an Android Twitter app has a great User interface.

TweetBot includes the ability to choose a list to display as your main timeline, excellent notifications and a beautiful interface, and

OpenBeak (http://orangatame.com/products/openbeak/) and Blaq (http://www.allblaqeverything.com/download/) are apps for BlackBerry phones, among many others.

TweetCaster (http://tweetcaster.com/features) has some additional features, like multiple accounts, post on Facebook, schedule tweets, photo uploading, Twitter trends etc. and the FREE version is adequate for normal users.

TIP: More than 425 million monthly active users used *Facebook* mobile products in December 2011(Source: http://newsroom.fb.com). The numbers will be much higher in 2012 so you'd better have a mobile strategy ready!!

> *TIP:* Twitter announced on March 20, 2012 that Promoted Tweets will be appearing in the timelines of mobile app users, even if they don't follow that brand advertiser. Source: http://bit.ly/twtmobileapp. The mobile ads are coming so get ready to allocate your budget for it.

Some other social network sites that can be accessed from your mobile phone are:

- *Meet Moi* (http://www.meetmoi.com): This website is an online dating platform for people seeking dates discreetly. The main feature of this resource is that you get contacts of other people looking for dates in your area. Then you can get in touch with them, chat, share pictures, and take things forward, all from your mobile device.

- *Treemo* (http://www.treemo.com): This online mobile community lets you share pictures, video, songs and express your creative side to the whole world.

Now whether these smaller sites and apps will last for long in a market dominated by Twitter and Facebook is a matter for the future. But the ever-expanding market has sufficient space for the small players to co-exist with the big shots so the end-users will have a host of choices when going for social media on mobiles for a long time to come.

And that's not all you can do on mobiles, as far as using online social channels is concerned.

1. *You can participate* in online polls, social contests, and give ratings and reviews whenever you want.

2. *Updating blogs from mobile devices is also a possibility* if you are into mobile blogging. So, whether you are enjoying a game of football or taking a break from work, you can get busy with your fingers and create new matter for your blog. Most blog entries are supported by email (using a POP3 client) and text messaging. But the most popular blogging platforms, such as WordPress (http://iphone.wordpress.org/)

and iBlogger (http://illuminex.com/iblogger/),
are now available in modified form for mobile devices such as the iPhone.

For the BlackBerry you have WordPress for BlackBerry (http://blackberry.wordpress.org/), which makes the job of writing and editing posts, along with managing comments, a breeze. If you are using Android-powered phones, you have two options: the wpToGo (http://danroundhill.com/wptogo/), which allows you to upload full size images and the PostBot (http://code.google.com/p/postbot/), which is a Google app allowing you to post to WordPress publications.

Then there is the moBlog application for Windows mobile devices (http://sampath.wordpress.com/moblog/). This application is optimized to consume minimum system resources while running on Windows Mobile devices.

So, all these apps, along with a phone having a QWERTY keypad, can make blogging on the go fun and easy.

3. *View and share videos*. Most modern phones are equipped with video cameras that can help you record hours of video on your phone. And smartphones even allow you to upload these or other videos to various social sites such as YouTube and Facebook. This can of course be done by using email services. But nowadays, mobile video sharing services such as Qik

(http://qik.com/) can also help you post videos directly from your phone to the sites.

This is possible because live streaming is a reality of 3G and 4G networks. If videos buffer, then there is really no joy in viewing them.

In addition to this, you have various mobile sites which add to the lure of using the Internet on mobile devices. They may not exactly be social sites, but they do help to draw in the crowds and are linked to social sites via embedded links. So, a lot of people who start using social sites on mobiles may have actually visited these commercial or retail sites at first and then become a fan on Facebook or a follower on Twitter.

But if you take a look at the list of top mobile sites (http://www.marketingcharts.com/interactive/top-10-mobile-phone-websites-march-2012-21684/), ranked according to share of visits in the US market, you will find that there are quite a few social sites in there. This goes a long way in further illustrating the type of impact of social media on mobile usage and vice versa.

THE REAL MOBILE SOCIAL MEDIA

Despite what you have just read through, in most countries social media on mobile is still in a phase of growth and evolution. In countries like Japan, however, social media is almost all mobile! Surprising as it may sound, a Mobile Marketing Data Labo (http://mmd.up-date.ne.jp/) study revealed that more than 75% of social media users in Japan access their accounts only from their mobiles and not laptops or PCs.

If you didn't get the point being made here, focus on the word *only*. This is of course possible because 3G networks form 95% of the market and about 85% of all users purchase data plans from these networks. This is a more advanced mobile market than anywhere in Europe or US and the use of social media on mobile devices here truly speaks a thing or two about the future trends.

But perhaps more of a surprise is the fact that a majority of social media users prefer Japanese sites rather than international ones such as Facebook or Twitter. So you have a site like mixi (http://mixi.jp/) with 17 million users as compared to Facebook, with only 1.4 million users! This may be put down to the fact that most of the bigger social platforms are English language based, but the reality is something deeper.

The reason why indigenous social channels are popular in Japan is because they have successfully integrated gaming into the user experience. When they are logged on to the Internet via mobile, 60% of Japanese users play games. This is the pulse which has been picked up by sites such as Gree (http://gree.jp/?action=login). Facebook and Twitter offer content exchange but gaming is not their USP by any stretch of imagination.

One more reason behind the dominance of mobile phones in the realm of social media in Japan is the fact that sites such as mixi offer premium content to users without billing them separately for it. The charges are added to the mobile bills, thus making the entire transaction hassle-free for the end users. This model even led to a misunderstanding on the part of the media that Twitter would start a paid subscription service for viewing Tweets from certain users. But these were quickly dispelled by Twitter, much to the delight of Twitter followers in Japan.

It may not be correct to assume that other markets will grow in the same way as this. But nevertheless, the Japanese market reflects the actual synergy between social media and mobile phones, something which may also come true for European and American markets. This can happen when hardware and software technology along with Internet accessibility and speed will be at its very best. The key takeaway here though is that, the more advanced the mobile market, the greater the usage of social media on mobile devices.

WHAT'S IN IT FOR BUSINESSES?

So, where does all this leave you, the business owner? For starters *it leaves you with the need to engage in social media more aggressively,* so as to gain first-mover advantage. All signs point to the fact that mobile development will be the next step forward in social media. So, it greatly increases the need to use social channels for marketing.

You can extend your product and services to your present and potential customers via a device which is closest to them 24x7. If your original purpose of getting into social media was to be a part of conversations and promote the creation of user-generated content that could favor your brand, then mobile phones have just opened up a gold mine for you.

So, without a shade of doubt you need to concentrate on social media development focused on the mobile phone and smartphones. This may be quite challenging because you will require a team capable of handling the various apps of the iPhone, the Android phones, the BlackBerry, the Windows Mobile, and Symbian phones. Now recruiting or training a team of employees with specific skill sets for each of these mobile platforms may be difficult, but you have to try.

Because if you focus on a social media niche and neglect others, you may be missing out a major benefit: the creation of inter-platform buzz. Say you're very active on Facebook on mobile devices but not so active on Twitter. This will create a void because when a Twitter user and a Facebook lover interact, their conversation about you will not be productive because while one can rave about your social savvy nature the other will have very little idea of why you rarely update your Twitter account.

The same goes for not tailoring your content for accessibility from various phones and smartphones. This obviously starts with having a dedicated URL for mobile browsers for your blogs and websites.

Very soon the day is coming when people will not even visit company websites to make purchase decisions. They will decide and, if possible, purchase within their social contacts. And mobile devices will play a crucial role in that revolution of distributed shopping as well, by shortening the time required to access peer-generated content and execute purchase decisions.

And companies have already recognized this fact. Coca Cola USA has started social media and mobile marketing together to bring the customer closer to the brand. In its program known as My Coke Rewards (http://www.mycokerewards.com/home.do), people are encouraged to use their mobile phones for entering the unique code under the bottle cap of its various soft drink brands, which can then fetch various loyalty rewards. The logic provided by the company is that users cannot be expected to carry a bottle cap all day long till they can access their PC. How true! How mobile!

In May of 2009, Taco Bell, the US fast food giant, launched a dedicated iPhone app for their customers. The basic aim of this app (http://www.ignitesocialmedia.com/taco-bell-social-media-marketing-example/) is to help people find products under $1 and also locate stores nearest to the user.

Even lingerie retailer Victoria's Secret has integrated their website VS Pink in the social domain, by taking it to the mobile realm. The website (http://vspink.mobi/) provides a remarkable level of detail and encourages visitors to interact, share, and download.

And social media marketing on mobile is being facilitated even further by the presence of the right mobile analytics. These analytics give you the power to measure:

- mobile marketing campaigns via social channels,

- visitors to your mobile website, and

- mobile applications created specifically for your business.

This is really important because traditional social media analytics cannot work for mobile social-media measurement. Most popular social analytics tools like Omniture and Google Analytics use Java tags to collect necessary data. But most mobile browsers do not work well with Java scripts. Even cookies that are used to measure website traffic are not retained by mobile phones, and so conventional analytics are rendered useless.

Some of the most popular mobile-specific analytics are:

Bango (http://bango.com/mobileanalytics/default.aspx): The best aspect of this tool is measuring mobile social media apps. They can be used to track events on any platform such as BlackBerry, iPhone, etc. This gives you a better understanding of what your customers are doing across all platforms.

AdMob (http://analytics.admob.com/home/): This resource is specifically targeted to measure the performance of your mobile website. Understanding your visitors, evaluating your traffic sources, and improving site performance can become easier once you start using this tool.

Localytics (http://www.localytics.com/): The USP of this site is "real time analytics for mobile apps." So, real time metrics can help you react to situations promptly and also make changes to your mobile social media strategy quickly. Data gathered here can also be analyzed with other tools.

LOOKING AHEAD

Technically speaking, you do not need to look that far ahead into the future to judge the importance of social media on mobile. Whatever we have discussed so far is more than enough to suggest that the future of social is more mobile than anything else! But the most pertinent example of the mobile-specific growth of social media, which is bound to continue in the future as well, is the rise of location-based social networks for mobiles.

The main offering of these sites is that you can let others know where you are all the time, play games based on location, and, of course, keep a constant connection with your friends. Some of these sites are:

- *Foursquare* (http://www.foursquare.com): This is the leading location-based social network at present, with more than 450,000 members. Users update their current location to friends by *checking in* with a smartphone app or text message. Foursquare accounts can also be connected to Twitter and Facebook accounts. It works for all smartphones and uses GPS tracking to pinpoint your location.

- *MyTown* (http://booyah.com/): This application is based around local shops, bistros, and other hangouts. Users check in and get points for moving up levels and unlocking virtual rewards, and they earn coins to buy their favorite location in the game. There are supposedly close to 1.4 million people hooked on this application, and users typically play it for 70 minutes a day on average.

- *RoamTribe* (http://www.roamtribe.com): This is an iPhone app that can make traveling a lot more fun, or at least this is what it promises to do. You can recommend your favorite places to others and also get valuable insights from experienced travelers before embarking on a vacation. You can also share the same with your Facebook friends.

So, the need for you to be proactive and harness the power of social media on mobile perhaps need not be stressed further. A recent study by Ruder Finn (http://www.prnewswire.com/news-releases/new-study-shows-intent-behind-mobile-internet-use-84016487.html) reveals that Americans spend nearly 3 hours a day on their mobile devices. And what are they doing in that4 ptperiod? Well, they are on the Web, socializing or not. And so you must be there too with your brand, products, and services. In fact, this study also found out that about 91% of people use the mobile Web to access social channels, as opposed to 79% who access social channels from the PC or laptop. In addition,

- 45% post comments on social websites,
- 43% connect with friends, and
- 40% are sharing content, while
- 38% are sharing photos.

If you want to be where the buzz is, isn't mobile social media the place to be?

CHAPTER 11: THE ACTION PLAN

This chapter is what you tear from this book and fill-up to ensure long-term success of your social program.

Social media is a relatively new and ever-changing field, so keep this at your desk at all times to keep you from getting distracted from your goals. You will still be open to new things coming up in social media, but this will keep you focused on how to integrate new tools without moving away from your final goal.

Ajay Tejwani

Enterprise Strategy

Put your long term startegy statement here.

Social Media Strategy

Put your social media strategy statement here.

Social Media Goals and Objectives

Define Goals and Objectives for your social program.

Social Media Change Management Plan

Identify your stakeholders and other teams that would be involved in implementing your goals and objectives.

Social Media Execution Plan

Allocate budget, time, IT investment and resources that will be needed to accomplish your goals.

Social Media Metrics

| Based on your goals and objectives, list out what you will need to measure as part of your social program. | Also list any tools and technology needed to get the right metrics. |

Social Media Dashboard

| Create visual presentation of your metrics that can be consumed by the stakeholders. | Take multi-tiered approach, from very high level dashboard to a detailed dashboard. |

Feedback to Improve the Strategy

| Identify the different channels from where you will receive the feedback. | Consolidate the feedback and feed it back into the Social Strategy. |

196

SOCIAL MEDIA ACTION PLAN FOR SMEs

Created by: Last Update:

Approving Manager:

Team Members:

GOALS/OBJECTIVES

What are the business goals you hope to achieve by using social media? What are your public relations goals (if any or n/a)? What are your community goals (if any or n/a)?

WHY SOCIAL MEDIA?

What are your reasons for using social media? What are the types of content you'll provide? Will you ask your community to provide content for you?

PERFORMANCE METRICS

What are the outcomes and outputs you would like to see from Social Media efforts? *(If you can't measure it, you can't control it.)*

OTHER MARKETING EFFORTS (E.G., EMAIL, PAID DISPLAY, ADWORDS, PRINT, MASS MEDIA, ETC.)

LIST OF COMPETITORS

TARGET MARKET

Who is/are the intended audience(s) for the social media program? What are their demographics (gender, race, age, employment status, location, etc.)?

LIST OF PEOPLE INVOLVED IN THE SOCIAL PROGRAM

Point(s) of contact from your company involved in this project and their roles.

Name	Email address	Main Role	Will they need training?	Facebook Personal	Facebook Business	Twitter

PRESENCE ON OTHER SOCIAL SITES ACCOUNT(S):

Yelp, StumbleUpon, Digg, Delicious etc.

SPECIAL OFFERS FOR YOUR FANS/FOLLOWERS:

MOBILE MARKETING DETAILS:

MOBILE WEBSITE (IF ANY):

EXISTING SEO/SEM KEYWORDS (IF ANY):

YOUR WEBSITE:

BRAND NAME FOR SOCIAL SITES:

INDEX

Download all the links in this book at
thesocialmediaactionplan.com/links